Together We Rise

Ravenwolf

First Paperback Edition: August 2021

ISBN: 978-1-68524-580-1 (print)
ISBN: 978-1-68524-599-3 (e-book)

Hyperbole Publishing
www.houseofravenwolf.com

Stories of Hope, Love & Empowerment

Your Greatest Days Are Yet to Come

Don't tell me that love isn't meant for you, that
you're meant to be alone, that you're not
lovable, or even that it's too late for you.
None of that is true.
No one – not one of us – is too broken, too old,
too lost or too anything else to love ourselves
or for someone else to love us.
I know it's easier to believe all the bad stuff that
maybe you've heard for so long, but it's time to
break the cycle and change your mindset.
You are lovable.
You are worthy of love ... from yourself and
from others.
It's never too late for love to find you or for you
to start a new chapter.
If you're stuck in the darkness unable to find
the light, I'm holding out my hand ...
You can do this.
You're worth it.
You deserve to be happy, to be loved, to be at
peace.
All those things you've been telling yourself for
so long?
They're not true.

Let go of the past: it was a lesson, not a life sentence.

Where you've been doesn't define you – the scars, flaws and mistakes only tell part of your story.

Pick yourself up and decide you're done being a victim, finished feeling sorry for yourself and that you can make the choice to be happy.

I'm not going to tell you that it will be easy or painless, but I will tell you that it will be worth it, every step of the way.

I know you've been beaten down, hurt and lied to ... but that's over now.

I know your heart has been broken so many times you don't believe love is possible, but it is.

You've got a million reasons not to believe in yourself, love or the future, and I get that.

But all it takes is one.

Make a choice.

Stay down or choose to get up and start clawing your way out of the struggle.

Don't give up, give in or accept defeat ... you're better than that.

Your best days are still ahead of you ... you just have to start believing ...

In yourself, in love, in hope, in that what I'm telling you is true.

Your best kiss, hardest laughter, deepest love and happiest days are yet to come ...

It may not be easy, but you can do it if you choose to.

So, take my hand and let's find a way back to the light.

If you don't believe, take some of my belief ... I believe in you enough for the both of us.

You were meant for more.

It's time to remember the magic you lost along the way and the dreams you once had.

They're waiting for you, just around the corner.

Your wings are ready ... dig deep and find your courage.

It's time to fly, Darling.

Life Is About Moving Forward

I know there are days when you wake up and
the whole world seems to be crashing down on
your shoulders.
Close your eyes and take a deep breath.
You don't have to have it all figured out or even
know where the day will take you.
There's always going to be those days when
you can't seem to get anything right and
everything just piles up.
You don't have to conquer it all at once.
Stop focusing on the whole weight of your
world and take it one step at a time ...
Baby steps if you have to.
Every one of us is a mess sometimes – we all
have moments where we just want to cry – and
if you need to, just let it out.
Tackle each thing, job and task one at a time
and keep moving forward.
Some days, you'll feel as though you can do
anything and other days, you'll put your keys in
the refrigerator.
That's just life – some good days, some bad
days and some days that make you want to
quit.
Don't.

You'll never be perfect, but the great thing is ... you don't have to be.

Don't put unrealistic expectations on yourself and then let the worry of how you'll get it all done stress you out.

Most importantly, stop being in a hurry all the time to do all the things and get everywhere super-fast ... you'll miss some of the greatest little moments if you're zooming through trying to conquer life without stopping.

Never get too busy doing and forget to live along the way.

Do the things, get the jobs done, be efficient ... But more than that, notice the small things: the smell of a fresh morning dew, the beauty of the world around us, the laughter of small children playing.

That's the stuff of memories that you'll miss if you're in a constant task tizzy.

Don't neglect them – they're important – but don't neglect yourself, either.

Take the time to fill your heart and soul with the joy that replenishes you.

So, yes, you're going to be a mess some days, and sometimes, you'll be figuring it out as you go ... just keep moving forward. Do what you can, how you can, when you can.

Most of all, don't stop living and enjoying your life.

After all, what good is it to conquer the world if you don't take the time to enjoy it along the way?

Each day is a new opportunity to start a new chapter.

Keep going ... you'll get where you need to be when you need to be there.

It just takes a little time, effort and patience sometimes.

You got this.

A Queen Turns Pain into Power

She hasn't had the easiest life – in fact, it has often brought her to her knees.
While the people she meets would marvel at her strength, they don't know the struggles she's endured to become the woman she is today.
Yes, she's found a way to dig deep and rise above the fire that once threatened to tear her apart.
She still cries in the shower sometimes and fights to keep it together ... but she knows now what it takes to keep moving forward.
There are still days when she battles just to keep a smile on her face, but she's become used to that – she's a fighter.
She's walked through the fire, risen from the ashes and done what she had to do to survive the hard times ...
And she doesn't regret any of it.
She learned from the toughest challenges what it takes to do more than simply survive.
She wants to thrive and be happy, most of all.
She is done living day to day and heartbreak to heartache.

She's determined to rise above and find her wings again.

She's not a princess, a damsel in distress or a starry-eyed girl in search of love.

She's turned her pain into power and transformed herself into a queen ...

Never settling, accepting no excuses and no longer allowing anyone to mistreat or disrespect her.

She'll admit that she doesn't have all the answers and she doesn't always know what her days will bring ... and she's more than okay with that.

She's gritty, courageous and full of zeal.

Maybe she falls and stumbles, perhaps she takes some wrong turns and makes some bad decisions.

But she owns her mistakes and appreciates life in the small moments of beauty that she sees all around her.

To her, strong is the new pretty, and she's not out to impress or win anyone's approval.

She's happy living her best life and spreading sparkle, love and sass wherever she goes.

Oh, and one more thing ...

When they try to call her "princess," "hot," or "sweetheart," she'll just smile at them and

remind them in the most charming way she
knows how ...
"I think you're mispronouncing 'queen,'
Darling."
And with a smile and a wink, they realize that
she's one of a kind.
Queens aren't born, they're made.
With her crown forged in the fire, she was born
to be great.

I'm Coming Back

I looked in the mirror and exhaled deeply.
It had taken me a long time to get to this point
... Blood, sweat and tears?
No, so much more than that.
I'd been beaten down, dragged through the
mud and thrown into the fire ... and that was
just the start.
I made the classic mistakes of giving my heart
to all the wrong people in all the wrong ways,
and every one of those broken roads cut me a
little deeper and taught me a little more ...
About who I was, where I'd been and what I
wanted.
Sure, I hated having my heart broken time and
again, but I would never change a thing about
all the wrong turns I'd made.
They led me to exactly where I was meant to
be: standing here, in front of the mirror,
beginning to recognize a person I had lost a
long time ago ... me.
I thought by forging an identity in the people I
loved and losing myself in them, I'd be happier,
and the love would be stronger ...
And it never was.
Turns out, that's not the way love works.

Real and lasting love doesn't ask a person to change into something other than who they are, and I've finally started making my way back to myself, where I never should have left to begin with.

It's been a long journey full of bumps and bruises, falls and failures, but I'm finally starting to recognize the person I've been trying to find and love all along.

Smiling, I pulled my hair back and swiveled my hips into a fun pose.

"Girl, you've been gone way too long! Let's never do that again ..."

I laughed loudly and beamed.

Sometimes, you gotta go through the hard times, try to love the wrong people and learn the difficult lessons to find your way.

It's been hard, it's been painful, it's been full of sadness ...

But it's all been worth it.

I'm on my way home to a better, stronger, happier version of myself, and it's a great feeling.

I'm turning my pain into power, my struggles into my strength and most of all,

My lessons into reasons.

I needed to turn my setback into my comeback
– and here I am, wiser, stronger and with a
deeper love of myself than I've ever known.
I took one last look in the mirror, grinning
broadly.
"I sure did miss you, girl. Let's go remind them
world why you're amazing."
And with a wink and a laugh, I kept moving
forward on my journey ...
This time, I'm doing it my way.

The Best Love Makes You Better

When I met you, I thought I had it all worked
out.
I knew where I was going and had everything
under control ... or so I thought.
Truth is, I didn't even have a clue.
You turned right into left and upside down into
right side up.
You made me want to be better ...
Not just for you, but for me as well.
For both of us, for our relationship, for our
future.
You changed what I thought would make me
happy and what made me smile.
We talk about nothing for hours and laugh
about the silliest things.
Conversations about deep feelings and the
hysterical kind of laughter that makes my side
hurt from laughing so hard.
You showed me that being the best version of
myself is what matters the most –
And what you truly loved about me.
You're my best friend who thinks my jokes are
funny ... even when I know they're kinda
cheesy.

You're my soulmate who walks beside me in our life, holding my hand every day
You're my lover who excites me with each kiss and scintillates my soul with every touch.
You're my daily reminder of how amazing life can truly be ...
When I wake up and see your face smiling at me, it just makes me realize –
You made me believe again ...
In magic, in love and in you.
I wouldn't change a thing.
I love us for all the things we've been, what we are now and what we will always be.
Most of all because you'll always be mine ...
Forever and always.

A Butterfly with Bullet Holes

They judged her because they thought they
knew her – only, they had no clue who she
really was.

She was a rare creature who had managed to
fly high in spite of all the things that had tried to
take her down.

The world would see her failures and her falls,
thinking she'd stay down on rock bottom.

What they didn't know about this woman was
that the same fire that had tried to destroy her
had also forged her courage and bravery.

She wasn't content to let the storms douse her
fiery will – far from it.

She always knew who she was and what she
could do, and she was never going to allow her
failures to define her.

Amidst the chaos that was once her life she
had found her wings. And despite everything
stacked against her, she started to learn to fly.

No one gave her a chance and she was
accustomed to that – she had never been
given anything in her life except a choice to
fight her way out of the anguish she once
knew.

She earned each step she took and bore the signs of that strength: scars, scratches and bruises that forged her indomitable spirit.

Sure, she fell from the skies more times than she could count and had to pick herself up much of the time ...

But she preserved because her story never gave her any other choice.

Day by day, step by step, she began to soar higher with each opportunity ...

Flying high with the courage, fire and fight that characterized exactly who she was ...

And with the grace of the beautiful soul that she was, she just kept smiling and shining ...

For she was one of those remarkable people you never forget.

Always strong, beautiful and free ...

Now, she was flying high too ...

And she never looked back.

Safe and Free and Happy

Hey, you ... Yes, I'm talking to you.
I know you're exhausted trying to get
everything done every day and it never seems
to end ... All those things that you're trying to
do every day?
They're not going anywhere.
Don't get so busy rushing through life that you
forget to live.
Life and all its moments are calling to you, just
hoping you'll see them.
Perhaps you've gotten so caught up in the
hustle and bustle and missed the joy of the
moments.
Stop.
Breathe.
Take back your life; stop letting your life control
you.
Don't be that person who looks back at the end
of their life and wishes they'd done all the
things, experienced all the moments and truly
lived.
This is your chance to turn the page and start a
new chapter ...
Make it a story worth telling.
Live in the moment.

Put your phone down, lift your head up and start seeking the beauty of this world.

Lose yourself in a glorious sunset with its dying hues of amber rays.

Breathe in the warm winds of a wonderful afternoon.

Experience wet puppy nose kisses.

Revel in the laughter of small children.

Go barefoot in the stream.

Take a road trip to nowhere with your best friend.

Sing in your car as loud as you can.

Dance in the kitchen.

Lose yourself in the music.

We spend so much of our lives sweating the small stuff that we forget to notice the little miracles that are all around us every day … and there's true beauty in those details.

Let's stop complaining, gossiping, wishing, wanting and asking for something bigger and better, and let's love what we have.

Enjoy your blessings and appreciate the joys that perhaps have escaped you for far too long.

Stop fretting about what has been and start looking forward to the possibilities that lie ahead.

And before you can tell me that you can't, I'll remind you that you can ...

But you have to want to become more, and you must believe in your future.

If you don't think it's possible, take my hand and let's do it together.

I don't know what tomorrow holds, but I do know with love in our hearts, passion in our souls and courage in our spirit, there's nothing we can't do.

The opportunities are limitless for you and me.

Are you ready to find your magic again?

It's been waiting for you this whole time.

Now, it's time to believe ...

In you, your heart and your dreams ...

It all starts with you.

You got this.

She made the choice a long time ago to never surrender to the problems and challenges that tried to bring her down.

She never set out to become strong, tough or brave, her story simply never gave her another option.

She's always done whatever it takes to make it wherever she's trying to go, but she's never sold her soul or sacrificed her values to reach those goals.

She's not perfect, and she gave up trying to be a long time ago.

She's made her fair share of mistakes, wrong turns and bad choices, but that never dissuaded her from pressing forward.

She never asked, "why me?" She just found a way through the struggles ... every time.

She's more than just a simple woman, though you may not realize that at first glance.

She's a warrior spirit, with the soul of a dreamer and the heart of a lover ...

More than anything, she's been searching for peace and love since the very beginning.

She loves with all her heart – herself, her people, her life – and perhaps, one day, her "forever person."

She's never questioned the timing of life. Rather, she's learned to do the hardest thing of all: Trust.

Herself, her heart, life's timing ... all the things that she could have stopped believing in so long ago, but never did.

She's had her heart broken into a million pieces, and each time she picks them up bit by bit puts herself back together again ...

Each time better and stronger than before.

She's a complex person with simple needs, and she's never abandoned her desire to be happy in the things that matter.

No. She survives, but she's more than a survivor.

She's always kept her fire burning and her light shining brightly ... believing in herself throughout it all.

Maybe one day she'll rest ... but that time isn't now.

She still has much to do and an entire future full of possibilities ...

Falling in love with being alive every day. Strong, beautiful and free.

One day, she'll be in love with herself and her life, finally at peace and content ... perhaps, even more ...
And she can't wait.

When All That Really Matters Is That You're Together

No matter where life has led us,
Through the challenges and struggles,
Across the world and through the storms,
We still found our way back home, together.

We didn't always know where we were headed
Or even what we were doing sometimes,
All that I care about is that I did it all
With you beside me, holding my hand.

We've had our fair share of ups and downs,
Happiness and sorrow, but that's just life.
We always cherished our love or each other,
And we truly loved faithfully and honestly.

We've celebrated the milestones with joy
And we've enjoyed the small moments of life
Never forgetting each and every day,
To love each other along the way.

So, as I look into your eyes and my heart
smiles,
It's from a life spent by your side, in love,
Experiencing the best and worst

Holding the hand of my one true love ...

My best friend, my lover, my soulmate and
truth,
You've given me a lifetime of memories
And a heart full of love, and I smile.
I did it all with the best thing that's ever
happened to me:
You.

Here's to many more, my love.

Yours Is the Only Opinion That Matters. Be Gentle with Yourself

I learned a long time ago that everyone had an opinion of me, and whether it was true or not, it didn't matter.

I used to try to make everyone love me, win the hearts of strangers for reasons that didn't matter ...

And at the end of the day, none of that made me feel any better about myself.

In fact, it made me feel worse.

Living a lie to impress fake people for silly reasons ... and for what?

That's why I stopped all of that nonsense.

I'll never make everyone happy or even convince the world to love the real me.

What matters is what I feel when I look in the mirror and the love I have for myself.

Sure, I've got tons of flaws, imperfections and broken pieces, but that's how the light gets in.

I'll never regret anywhere I've been, people I've loved or choices I've made ...

That's the road that led me to become who I am.

Every scar tells a story, and every flaw has a meaning ... and they've made me who I am ...

A beautifully broken and wonderful mess who loves every part of her sometimes-chaotic life.

I've learned to appreciate what the world would call my imperfections.

That's my hard-earned character, built on the back of my struggles and forged from the fires of my failures ... and my subsequent rising again.

No, I don't have anything really figured out and some days, I'll put my keys in the freezer and the groceries in the coat closet.

Those quirks make me uniquely beautiful, and I've learned to appreciate them in all their flawed glory.

So, let people judge me for the path they don't know for the reasons they'll never understand ... I'm good with that.

I've built who I am for me, because of me, to become an even better me.

And I'm getting better, wiser and stronger every day.

It's a hard journey to self love, one I'm still making, but I'm getting better at it.

So, I'll keep doing my best and making the most of my chances and let the rest happen as it's meant to.

I'm happy chasing my dreams and living my life just the way I'm supposed to, the way that makes me happy ...
On my terms.
And really, there's nothing more that I could ever ask for than that.
My happiness is worth that ... and much, much more.

Sometimes "Goodbye" Is the Purest Forum of "I Love You"

I know you'll never forgive me for walking away from us, and that's okay, I'll have to live with that.

You've kept pushing me to fight for us, to hold on.

You said you thought we could make it work. But that's just it ... we have been down that road so many times before, and it never worked., not even a little,

We both tried with all our hearts and did all we could do, but together, you and I were toxic. We were magical in the very beginning – butterflies and passion catapulted our hearts to heightened sensations of love, desire and need – but somewhere along the way, we lost ourselves and each other, and it all turned dark.

There wasn't just one event or a single act, but a gradual turn, and slowly I felt bad and then worse.

I'm done trying to figure out what went wrong or how to fix us, because we are way past that now.

So, before we end up hating each other, I'm letting you go.

Not because I don't love you or that it's easy, it's just what my heart tells me is right.

We've tried everything, and I can't fight any more for something that I know isn't meant to be ... we are just oil and water, which tears my heart in two.

I hope, over time, you'll forgive me for loving you enough to let you go ...

It won't be easy for me either, but I know it's the right thing to do.

I know we won't be happy for a while as we lead newly separate lives, but we haven't been happy together for a while.

You'll blame me, hate me and make me the bad guy, and I'll have to live with that.

As I write these words with tears in my eyes, I know that some say that real strength lies in holding on ...

I now know that letting go is the hardest thing I'll ever have to do.

Maybe one day, you'll think of me and smile, but if you don't, that's okay, too.

I'm doing what I think is right for us both to be happy ...

Maybe we'll meet each other in the next life
and things might be different.
Until then, I'll miss you and wish you the best
... I'm taking my own road, and it'll be hard.
But I'll be fine ... I always am.
I know somehow and someday I'll end up
exactly where I'm meant to be, and so will you.
I'm not saying goodbye ... I'm saying I love
enough to let you go.
I hope one day you'll understand.

Beautiful, Powerful, Magical

Today, I woke up with the strangest idea.
I decided to let go of all those people who
didn't really try to be in my life and didn't see
my worth.
I realized that I'm amazing, and it's not my fault
they missed that about me.
I'm going to stop chasing attention, affection
and respect and go where the love is.
My people know me, care about me and love
me deeply in the ways I know I deserve.
Why do I need more when I have what I want?
I don't.
So, I'm going to stop chasing people for the
right reasons in the wrong ways.
If someone doesn't see my worth and value my
time, then I'll spend my energy on the people
who do.
I'm saying goodbye to the critics, the
judgmental and the pretenders.
I'm saying hello to my magic, my voice and my
power to do anything I set my mind to.
I'll never tell you that I have it all together,
because I wake up a lot of days wondering
where I put my phone or trying to drag myself
out of bed.

I'm a world-conqueror on my best days, and I'm a beautiful mess on my worst.

But I'm real, authentic and down to earth.

What you see is what you get, and I'll always tell it like it is ...

Which doesn't always make me everyone's favorite person.

Their loss.

I've got a lot of love to give and a passionate heart, and I'm always going to pour all of myself into anything I do and the relationships I have.

Maybe that makes me too much for some people, but then, those aren't my people.

So, I didn't wake up today thinking I was going to change the world – not even my own – but I'm ready to start taking the steps and making the changes that are long overdue.

I know it won't be an easy process, but the right kind of change isn't ever painless.

I'm letting go of the drama queens, the haters and the people who just don't make the effort.

I'm worth more than that.

I'm beautiful, I'm strong and I'm free ...

But more than that, I'm powerful and magical too ...

And I deserve to live my life free of criticism and judgement.

Maybe they'll care when they see me walking away, maybe they won't.

I'll be fine either way ... I always am.

No matter where my choices lead me or the road I have to take, I know I'll end up where I'm meant to be.

So, as I lie in bed and see the glorious rays of the morning sun peeking through the windows, I can't help but smile.

I'm finally setting myself free to become who I was always meant to be.

Today is going to be a really good day.

I Live Big, Don't Dare Try to Love Me Small

All my life I've been told who I should be, what I should wear or what I should look like.
I tried to do what I was told, but it just didn't take.
I was never happy fitting into their labels and boxes, so I stopped trying.
I realized that I'm unique, and I want more than to just do what everyone else is doing.
I can't and don't do anything small or halfway.
I'm not afraid to put myself out there and take risks.
Sure, I've been hurt more than my fair share, but I don't stop trying to love and be loved.
It's a risk I'm willing to take because the reward – love – is worth the price ... any price.
I know many would never agree with that, but it's my choice, and I'll take the chance without hesitation.
I've spent many sleepless nights crying myself to sleep or tossing and turning in bed, unable to rest because my mind wouldn't stop ...
But that's just part of it, and I accept that.
I refuse to stop living and stop loving because I've had my heart broken.

I learned from my mistakes, and I built higher walls around my heart, but I still give too much of myself ... that's just who I am.

I live every day to the fullest, I love with all my heart ...

And I don't plan on changing.

It's who I am – I can't love anything or anyone halfway.

So, if you think you're going to come into my life with some lackluster passion or part time friendship, think again.

I expect what I give, and I give it all.

I'm always there for my people and I always will be.

I wear my heart on my sleeve and I speak my mind ... that's just who I am.

When it comes to romance, I don't need grandiose promises or fancy dreams.

I yearn for real, authentic and genuine love: deep feeling, soul touching, heart stimulating and visceral emotional connection.

Anything less isn't enough for me.

I'm sure the world will shake its head in disapproval at the way I live and love, and they're welcome to pass judgment on me.

It doesn't mean I'll care or listen.

They don't know where I've been and don't know my reasons, so they don't have the right to think they know me ... because they don't. So, I'm going to keep charging hard into every day with everything I have, no matter how hard the challenges may be.

I was born to become more, and that's just what I'm doing.

Big heart, big hopes, big dreams ...

And it all starts with me.

I'll keep taking the chances for amazing love and wonderful friendships because, just like I always do, I'm going to keep loving hard and living with all my heart.

It's now or never,

So, I'm choosing now.

Moments Like These

When the still of the night is upon us,
And the serenity wraps us in its embrace,
As I watch your sleeping form
Nestled up to me, I couldn't ask for more.

In those moments, the world melts away,
And the cares and concerns of the day
Don't seem to matter anymore,
As I can think only of our love and you.

These are the times that I wish I could freeze,
Suspend time as we linger in love's grasp,
The quiet and still calming our hearts
As we are two souls connected as one.

All the thoughts, feelings and emotions
Just seemed to dissolve as we rest quietly,
Your motionless body next to mine,
My heart is full in the beauty of this moment.

It's the snapshots of these instants
That I'll look back on and always remember,
For these are the memories of our life
That will always mean everything to me ...
Forever and always, yours.

The Strongest Wings

She's battled the hardest fights life could throw at her, and the weight of the world weighs heavily.

She's only ever had herself to depend on, so she doesn't look to anyone else to help ease her burden.

Whatever you want to call her – broken, a mess, lost – she doesn't care, because she stopped worrying about what others thought a long time ago.

She's been to rock bottom too many times and picked herself up more times than she can count.

She's not trying to be strong, a survivor or anything else, she is just trying to keep going.

She's tired of suffering without an end in sight.

Truthfully, she found herself in the darkness when she couldn't find anything else – not even the light.

She didn't know how she'd survive the broken failure that was her life, but somehow, painfully, she did.

She clawed her way out of the abyss and slowly, she began to build her resolve.

It was never about flying high or succeeding to her, it was just about finding some peace in a world that never gave her a chance.

No one ever expected her to rise from the ashes, so when they saw her pulling herself out of the emotional wreckage of her life, they were stunned.

They didn't know her life or her story, nor did they know her reasons ...

They never knew that this scarred and flawed angel never wanted wings, she just wanted to breathe free.

Reeling from the pain and digging deep to find her courage, she uncovered the parts of herself that she never knew existed.

She wasn't trying to be a hero or a role model, she was just trying to survive a story that didn't give her any other choice.

She was broken.

She was lost.

She was counted out.

She rose again ...

And using the pain to fuel the fires of her passion, she became something else entirely.

A warrior forged in fire and scarred by pain, with the beautiful countenance of a woman who has walked through hell, she vowed to

never again let anyone hurt her so deeply ...
and just kept smiling.

As she broke free of the shackles of struggle
that once held her down, she gleefully stepped
into the light that had eluded her for so long ...
In that moment, she found herself, finally, at a
place she'd never known ... but had long
dreamt of ...

And as she stepped into the dawn of a new
chapter, out sprung wings she'd never cared a
thing to have, but yet, she was always meant
to possess.

And, mustering the courage and strength to fly
high, she finally reached that place she had
wanted to find for as long as she could
remember ...

A place she'd sought her entire life ...

Where she was, at least, free ... free to breathe
deeply and free to fly high.

So that's just what she did ...

And she never looked back.

A Thousand Things to Say to You, and a Thousand Reasons Not To

It's always the worst at night.
The endless thoughts about you, about us.
I wonder what you're doing, what you're thinking ... if you're thinking of me.
I wish I could stop my mind from drifting off to thoughts of you, but it happens every time.
Not so long ago, we were lost in each other's arms, and we had nothing but time and love.
I can't really say what happened or where we went wrong, only that it still hurts.
Most of all, I wish I could turn off my heart and not feel anymore ...
Not miss you, the times we had and the love we shared.
It seems so far away and so close at the same time.
I'm a furious mixture of emotions: I want to cry, scream and be numb at the same time.
I want to feel everything and nothing, it's almost maddening at times.
I close my eyes, and I can still see your smile beaming at me and the warm happiness those moments gave me.

My friends tell me to stop thinking about you and move on. Deep down, I know they're right, but my heart isn't ready to let go.

Honestly, part of me would try again if I had the chance, even though I know that's the wrong choice ...

Anything to feel that love and joy for a bit longer, it seems.

But then, I realize that the good times were always followed by the bad times.

There's been so many times I've picked up my phone to text you, only to erase the words without sending anything.

I used to share everything with you, and my first instinct is still to reach out and connect with you ...

But I know that's the worst thing I could do right now.

I need to focus my time and energy elsewhere before I do something I regret – like calling or texting you.

Why are nights always the worst?

Exhaling, I close my eyes and put my phone down.

I can get through this time, and I need to find my strength again.

I wasn't happy with you, but now I'm not happy without you ...

Almost like I'm stuck in between worlds.

It's going to be hard, but I have to let you go or I'll never be able to start living again.

I know you'll always have a place in my heart, and as I open my eyes, I know that I have to move on.

It won't be easy, it won't be fast, but maybe, finally, I can find some peace that I've been missing for too long.

Day by day, learning to live again.

That, for now, will have to be enough, until I get to a better place ...

So that one day, when I see your name or picture, my heart won't hurt or race ... it won't feel anything for you at all.

I'll get there ... one day.

I Won't Apologize for My Fire

I'll never apologize for how hard I love or how intense I am.

I'm passionate about everything I do and everyone I love – and that won't ever change.

I refuse to tone down, water down or filter my personality or passion for anyone who can't handle me.

I know I'm fiery, sassy and a bit spicy at times, but that's just part of my charm ...

I'm not asking anyone to like me.

I realize that I may be an acquired taste, and I'm good with that.

There have been a lot of people who left my life. Maybe they didn't always agree with who I am or what I said ... and I wish them the best while respecting their choice.

I don't want anyone in my life who doesn't want to be there, all in.

I'm real, genuine and authentic in everything I say and do, so you'll know exactly where you stand with me.

I don't mince words, play fake or pretend.

Life is too short to spend my time and energy chasing people for their affection, attention and approval when I don't need it or even want it.

I know there are people out there who will say I'm unlovable, hard to handle and opinionated, and they're right.

I speak my mind, I share my truth and I'm open and honest about what I think.

So, if anyone wants to label me, name call or write me off because they don't approve of my personality, that's their choice ...

It won't change how I live my life, what I do or how I spend my time.

I'll never ask for permission to follow my heart and burn brightly for the things that matter most to me: my loved ones, my passions and of course, love, in all its forms.

Yes, I've loved the wrong people and kissed the wrong frogs, but I learned from every bad choice, and I kept loving hard when there was love to be had.

I put all of my heart and soul into my love, and that will never change.

It causes me to get hurt more often than I'd like, but I'll take that risk every time ...

Because without putting yourself out there, you'll never know the love that could be yours ... And I'm greedy, I guess.

I want all the love from the people in my life, and I'm going to enjoy every minute of it.

So, if you were waiting for an apology from me for my attitude, my passion or my words, I hate to disappoint you.

I'll admit when I'm wrong, and I'll apologize when I should, but I'll never say I'm sorry for being who I am and what I love.

Being in my life is a choice, and maybe it's not for everyone, but the ones who stick around appreciate me for all the things the world says I'm too much of: passionate, feisty, opinionated, strong.

Maybe I'm not your cup of tea, but I know some like their coffee a bit on the strong side ... Just like me.

So, whether you like me or not, I will always be real and true to my word.

In a world full of fakeness, I'd rather burn passionately and honestly for who and what I am than to be like the rest.

I'm never going out like that.

My life, my rules, my happiness.

It's really pretty simple if you ask me.

Sometimes Days She Has No Idea How, but Every Day It Still Gets Done

She stares in the mirror, mustering every bit of her courage and strength to take on the day.
Wiping away the beginnings of a tear, she breathes in deeply.
It's been a long week – no, make that a long year – for her.
She halfheartedly laughed.
"It's been a long forever," she said with the faint semblance of a smile.
This was one of the days she just didn't know how she was going to make it through.
She'd been up most of the night, tossing and turning ... and thinking.
It was always the endless waves of thoughts that kept her awake that made her soul weary.
Instead of waking up refreshed from the few hours of sleep she'd often get, she just woke up worried ...
About what she had to get done, the details of her tasks and whatever else her mind could jam into that space in her head.
The easier days were becoming fewer and less frequent, and the obstacles life threw at her were getting bigger and harder to overcome.

Just once, she wished, she wanted to tackle a day with all the answers.

"Or at least some of them ..."

Wistfully, she fixed her hair as she dug deep to put on the brave face that she gave the world ... You know the one, where everyone thinks you're okay, but deep down ...

"You're just hanging on by a thread."

She grimaced as her mind raced forward to what her day had in store for her.

Her closest friends knew her struggles and were there for her as much as they could be, but she knew that when it came down to it, she was the one who had to figure out a way to get it done.

People would often say they admired her resolve and strong façade, and she'd smile and make a joke about it ...

Because they didn't know.

They had no idea the fire that she walked through every day just to survive.

They had no idea what it took for her to keep going when all she wanted to do was quit.

They had no idea how she just wanted to stay in bed and hide from the world some days ...

But she couldn't.

There were people who depended on her to show up and step up every day, so that's what she did ... without hesitation, without question.

She was so many things for so many people when she just wanted to be at peace.

Sometimes, there's a sort of weary that sleep can't fix, and that's where she was.

She needed her heart and soul to have time to recover from the wounds of her past ...

The broken hearts, the damaging pain, the forgotten promises.

She tried never to ask too much of anyone, because she'd learned the hard way that those expectations only ever led her to disappointment ...

And she'd been let down enough in her life already.

She didn't know if she could handle any more. From the moment she stepped foot into the world until she was finally able to catch her breath late at night, there was always something to do, a task to be handled, a problem to solve ...

And it could be overwhelming.

Truthfully, she couldn't tell you how she managed to do all the things she did, only that she amazed herself sometimes.

She looked in the mirror one last time, wiping away smudges from the edges of her lipstick.

"Perfect ..."

She chuckled quietly.

"Or at least as close as I'll ever get to perfect in this life."

She smiled, exhaled and put on her brave face.

It was just one of those moments in the life of a warrior woman –

Amazing, strong and brave.

Because that's just who she is and would always be.

And every day, in every way, she always finds a way.

Just another day in the life of a hero.

You Deserve to Be Reminded Daily of How Very Special You Are to Me

No matter how my day may go,
nor what challenges that face me daily,
there is always that moment,
one of many,
that makes me stop,
close my eyes and think of you.
A song, a sound or just a thought ...
all those little things that remind me of you and
what you mean to me.
When those moments happen, I fall into a
reflection of you, your love, and your
enchanting smile.
I smile as the warmth and beauty of your love
wraps around me.
We were both once broken in our own unique
ways, but together, we realized that we were
imperfectly perfect for each other.
The lasting love on my lips from your kiss
carries me through my day with peace as I
leave you every day to face the world.
I don't know much, but I do know this:
As you have reminded me of what life and love
can be, you deserve to be reminded how

beautiful you are ... how very much you are
loved and how very special you are to me.
That much I will do, gladly, daily and forever –
from my heart to yours,
for the rest of our lives.
I love you.

A Part of Me Died When You Didn't Fight for Me, but All of Me Came Alive When I Had to Fight for Me

I thought you would always be the one I could count on who would stand up for me when things got tough.
I'd always believed you would fight for me because of how you felt about me.
Turns out, I was wrong.
While I know we had some rough times of late, our relationship had a lot of truly beautiful moments too ...
Or had you forgotten those, too?
When I needed you most, when things were the hardest ... you just turned your back on me.
I don't think I've ever been so hurt in my life.
I just couldn't believe the one person that I thought would always be there ... wasn't.
You just chose to walk away rather than fight for me, for us?
I ask myself a million questions trying to understand how you could do that ... and honestly, I don't know.
I may never know.
Maybe you didn't feel as strongly about me as you claimed, maybe something changed ... or

maybe you just fed me some words to make me believe we were the real thing.

I don't know. I'm just so hurt – I'm beyond pain, I'm numb.

I don't know where to turn or what to think, I'm completely lost.

This wasn't supposed to be how things were meant to turnout.

Part of me always believed you were the one and that my search was over ...

And now I'm just feeling dumb as you left me holding pieces of my broken heart.

But when everything came crashing down around me, you were nowhere to be found ...

So, I did what I never thought I could do and stood up for myself.

I fought for me when I didn't even think I had that kind of strength.

Sometimes, your story doesn't give you a choice, and that's exactly where you walked out on me ...

So, I did whatever I had to do to survive.

It's hard, I'm not going to lie – there are so many days when I want to quit – but I'd rather be out here struggling by myself than depending on someone who walks out when things get hard.

I'm done with that.
I'm sure you have your reasons and excuses,
but you never even bothered to explain it to me
... The one person you should have told first,
you didn't even think I was worth the effort.
I guess it's better to find out now than many
years down the road, but it still hurts all the
same.
I know I'll be fine eventually, because your
cowardice showed me a strength I didn't know
I had.
I'm strong enough, brave enough and
courageous enough to pull through this with my
head held high.
Maybe you walked out when the going got
tough,
But the toughness just made me get going.
I guess I should thank you for showing me the
way back home to myself, but I don't know that
I'll ever forgive you for what you did to me.
Doesn't really matter because I'm in a better
place now.
Where you left a girl to fend for herself without
a thought to how she'd make it,
There now stands a strong woman ...
With a heart of gold and a fiery spirit.
Some warriors are born ...

This one was forged in the fire.
I was made for this ...
Strong, beautiful and finally free.

Life Can Be Scary, but It Can Be Beautiful Too

I know you've been living day to day for too long, just trying to find your way.

It's exhausting, I know ... but you've been existing for so long that you've forgotten how to live ... and I mean truly live – outside the box, doing the little things that you used to do that made you happy.

Somewhere along the way, you stopped doing the things that filled your soul and brought you joy.

Maybe life got you down, you went through some hard times – it's easy to lose your way.

But I'm here to tell you that you need to go start finding yourself again.

It doesn't always have to be big adventures or extravagant trips; the little moments matter every bit as much.

When's the last time you truly stopped rushing and lived in those moments?

Appreciated the beautiful sunset.

Stood in awe of a star filled sky.

Were kind to a stranger.

Petted a rambunctious puppy.

There's beauty all around us, each and every day ... but if we never take the time to appreciate it, then we've forgotten what it means to live.

Stop putting off those things you've been meaning to do.

Write a poem, any poem.

Draw a sketch.

Kiss your favorite person.

Enjoy a long squeezing hug.

Dance in the kitchen.

There's immeasurable joy in being able to sit back and say, "I did that. I created something."

That's your legacy, that's the magic you've forgotten along the way.

The day and its tasks will always be there.

If you can only take a few moments a day, seize them and enjoy the beauty you've been overlooking.

Stop existing and start living.

You know, it won't solve any problems, but you might just be surprised what will happen when you adjust your perspective just a bit.

Don't be a person who looks back over their life and wishes they had done this or experienced that.

Your time is now.

Live. Create. Experience. Lose yourself in the beautiful moments that have been waiting for you.

You can't change the past and tomorrow is unknown, so make the most of today.

What are you waiting for?

Life in all its beauty is there, just around the corner.

Tell your people that you love them.

Embrace it all before it's too late.

Make today the start of a new chapter ...

Because in the end, your happiness, your life, your choices – all come down to you.

And I know you're capable of more.

This is your time to shine, Darling.

I thought it had it all figured out until you came into my life.

You said everything I wanted to hear, did all the right things and swept me off my feet.

It seemed too good to be true, but I wanted so much to believe in you and love ... that I did.

A whirlwind romance had me floating ... until the parts of our love story started to unravel.

The magic stopped and the butterflies went away and soon I was left fighting for a relationship so unhappy that I didn't even know what I was fighting for anymore.

I tried to see past the fights, the anger and the disrespect, but it just became too hard.

I realized I was fighting for my happiness, and it didn't feel good anymore – none of it.

Heart in pieces, I walked away carrying what I had left of my self-respect and dignity ...

Crying every step of the way.

You acted as though you cared and told me all the ways you'd change, but I soon learned actions speak louder than words ... for your actions never changed.

I tossed and turned in bed trying to analyze what went wrong, if it was my fault and what I could have done differently ...

And all that did was cause more pain and bring back more hurtful memories.

I did what I had to do to survive – I moved on. You made it a battle every step of the way, and I've had to do the things I thought I would never have to do ... disappear to you altogether, because "goodbye" wasn't an answer you were willing to accept.

I'm done being scared and looking out the window, wondering if you're going to show up. That's not living.

I'm putting the past – and us – behind me, and I'm not going back there.

I'm looking forward to the future ... I'm going to be happy again someday, somehow.

Maybe it won't be tomorrow or next week, but I'll get there.

Maybe it was love in its own way, I'll never know for sure, but I learned so much from our time that I'm growing into a stronger, wiser and better me because of it.

Some come into your life for a season, a reason or a lesson, and you were all three.

You've shown me what I want – and don't want – in love, and I know now that I'll never settle for less.

I've stopped dwelling on what went wrong, and I'm learning instead.

It's a painful lesson, but it'll make me better for it.

I'm turning the page and starting a new chapter of my life.

This one I'm calling simply ...

"Happiness."

I've been through some rough stuff, a past that tried to consume me and times that tried to destroy me.

Honestly, I don't know how I'm still standing sometimes.

All the wrong choices, dead ends and terrible loves I chased left me in pieces, every time.

You see, I learned that everyone isn't like me – they don't treat others fairly and they're not open and honest about what they want.

That was a lesson I learned in the hardest ways from the ones I tried to love ...

I gave away my heart too easily and had my hopes trampled way too often.

There was a time not so long ago that the failures of my life and the weight of the world brought me to my knees, and I didn't think I'd ever find my way out of that darkness.

I reached my breaking point ... and I broke.

But then, somehow, I kept going.

Broken, humbled and distraught, I still kept fighting.

With no one to turn to for help, I began clawing my way out of the mess that had become my life.

It wasn't pretty, and it hurt worse than anything I'd ever known, but somehow, I managed to find my way.

Despite the pain, I still had hope.

Despite my failures, I still believed.

Despite my heartbreak, I never gave up on love ...

For myself, my people and my future.

I never meant to come down the wrong roads and make all the worst choices, but now I know that's what I had to go through to become what I'm meant to be ...

And I wouldn't change anywhere I've been, because the things I learned have made me who I am.

The fires of struggles tried to consume me whole, but I'm stronger than that.

I became the fire which tried to vanquish me, and I rose out of the ashes.

These steps, no matter how small, were some of the hardest I've ever known.

But you know what?

I kept going, kept growing, kept burning brightly.

I had been through the worst, so I knew I could make it to the best.

So, yeah, I'm beautifully broken, if that's really a thing – I don't know how much beauty I saw down that painful road – but I'll take it ...

Because those cracks, those flaws that were forged under pressure?

That's how my light gets in.

No matter what lies ahead, I know there's nothing I can't handle.

I'm still here, standing tall, strong and proud.

I'm proud of what I've survived, proud of who I'm becoming, and most of all, I'm proud that I'm still pushing forward.

Maybe I don't have all the answers, but I do know this ...

No matter what happens or how hard things get ...

I got this ... and I always will.

You looked at me apprehensively, the fear
brimming in your eyes.

"What if I fall?"

I could see the emotions swirling in your face,
a mixture of excitement and curiosity.

You'd been through the ringer lately, and every
time you were almost on the other side of the
troubles, something else would pop up.

You couldn't win for losing, it seemed.

I knew that, deep down, you wanted to believe
in your dreams, in the possibilities that were
out there ...

But you had lost hope as life had knocked you
down, time and again.

So, as your eyes cried out for some positive
reassurance from me, I knew you needed me
to help you find your belief again ...

However long and hard that may be for you to
rediscover.

You'd been knocked down and dragged
through the fire so many times, I knew you
were afraid of being burned again.

It's hard to keep getting back up when you start
to lose hope.

Leaning forward, I took your hand and met your eyes with mine.

"Darling, I can't promise you the things you want to hear from me. I can't promise you that this will be easy, painless or successful. "

I paused and squeezed your hand tightly.

"I can promise you it will be worth it."

Exhaling, your frustration showed on your face. You wanted more from me.

You were tired of getting your hopes up, believing in something or someone, only to have it all fall apart.

Broken hearts and failed dreams are hard to swallow, though you'd done an amazing job of bouncing back, time and again.

There was this little bit of yourself that you kept holding onto, the part that didn't want to get let down again.

I knew you wanted to believe, you wanted to hope, you wanted to find the courage to fly.

It's been a hard road for you, through the pain, anguish and heartbreak ...

But you're still here, standing at the crossroads, looking to the skies and desperately searching for your strength.

You wanted to fly, you wanted to soar high like the amazing soul you have always been ... but life always had a way of letting you down, making it hard for you to believe in hope, yourself or the possibilities.

I watched your eyes scan the horizon momentarily before darting back to me.

I lowered my gaze and smiled warmly.

"This is your time. You've battled every day to get where you are, scrapping and clawing for everything you have ... and if you don't believe in yourself, your greatness ... take some of my belief, because I do. You can do this."

You closed your eyes and took a deep breath.

"And If I fall?"

I kissed your forehead and beamed.

"Oh, but my darling, what if you fly?"

I watched as you thought about what I said and, suddenly, a smile began to cover your face.

Nodding, you looked over at me.

"I can do this."

I laughed heartily.

"Of course you can, Darling ... you were born for this."

She Kept Trying, and That Was the Bravest Thing of All

She never thought of herself as brave, she just kept doing what she had to do to survive.

In fact, most days, she felt anything but brave as the worry about what could go wrong occupied her mind.

Like everyone else, she thought of bravery as the heroic tales of fighting injustice and saving the day ... and that wasn't her.

Far from it.

She did what she always had – she showed up, day in and day out, no matter how hard it was to get out of bed.

Regardless of how often she had cried in the shower, or how many times she wanted to scream in her car.

She was beautifully defined by those singular moments of ordinary heroism, the ones that many could muster. She kept showing up with a smile on her face even when she felt so far from happy.

In fact, just to get to this point in her life intact was a miracle unto itself – the broken roads, the failed loves, the painful disappointments ...

Everything that had happened to her would have destroyed most people ...

But then, she wasn't most people.

She was something altogether different: a brave, strong woman whose story never gave her any other choice.

It was either fail and stay down or rise up out of the ashes and keep going.

So, she did the bravest thing she knew to do:

She kept showing up, she kept trying, she kept loving.

She never lamented her broken past or her current struggles, for she was determined to build a brighter tomorrow.

She didn't know how she'd manage, but she always found a way ... that's just who she was.

Strong woman.

Proud dreamer.

Loving person.

Brave warrior.

She didn't have the answers and, most days, couldn't tell you how she'd make it through the day without crying or falling apart ...

But she did.

And she kept doing it.

Maybe she didn't realize it,

Maybe she didn't see it,

Maybe she didn't care ...

But to everyone around her for all the ways that truly matter, she was one of a kind.

Each and every day ...

She was brave, she was kind, and she was strong.

That's just who she was ...

Because she had the heart that wouldn't be denied ...

Now or ever.

In a word, she was brave.

I'm Proud of Who I Am Today and What It Took to Get Here

When they look at me and admire the woman I am, I know they have no idea what it took for me to get here, and that's okay.

Though I've been in some dark places and been down some bad roads, I wouldn't change a thing about who I am or where I've been.

I've made every mistake you can think of, and I've chased every bad love you can imagine, and yet, I'm still standing.

More than that, I'm thriving, growing and getting better every day.

Sure, it's hard to think back to the dark days when life brought me to my knees, and I didn't know how I'd ever survive ...

But I figured it out, I made my way and, somehow, I ended up on the other side of the storm intact.

I'll never tell you that I didn't cry mountains of tears, get down on myself or just wonder how I would survive, because I did all those things.

It's a hard thing when you're at rock bottom and all you've got is yourself to depend on ...

But that's how I forged my courage – in the flames that would have once tried to consume me.

I fought, I clawed and I struggled for every small victory and every little success that kept me going.

I kept climbing when I didn't have the strength, and I battled to become the woman I knew that I could be ...

And let me tell you –

I didn't think I'd make it most days.

But that's the beauty about writing your own story. I was the one holding the pen, and I refused to give in, give up or settle for less.

I knew what I wanted, and I realized what it would take, so I stopped complaining, whining and feeling sorry for myself, and I turned the page to a new chapter.

I picked myself up, I fought my way back from the bottom ... and I kept going.

So, yes, when I look in the mirror today, I'm very proud of the person I've become.

I earned my way here with every scratch, scar and bruise along the way.

It wasn't easy, painless or fast ...

But as I stand here smiling, standing tall and proud – through all the heartaches, the struggles and the pain – I remember the most important thing of all …

It was worth it, every step of the way, to become the woman I was always meant to be.

One Moment Can Change Your Life, One Love Can Change Your World

From the very first moment, we knew.
It wasn't just the things we said or did,
It was what we didn't have to say or do.
It's what we just knew.
When you belong with someone,
Every fiber of your being aches to be with them.
From the first hello, that sense of belonging became much more than a thought, a desire or a need ...
It became a necessity.
I often used to wonder how I'd know or what it would feel like,
but the truth is, I can't describe the beauty and amazing feeling you have when you find the one meant for you.
Words fail the wonder of that feeling, it eclipses all description and lies beyond any understanding ...
Because I just knew ... and the power of the truth lies far beyond anything words could describe.
I knew the answer before I could even ask the question, and while that may not make sense

to all, the ones who have been there will understand.

The glances that become conversations,

The kisses that become fire,

The moments that become memories.

There are countless ways that I love you and countless more reasons that I'm proud to be by your side.

I'll never let a day go by without reminding you how very much you're loved nor a time pass by where I don't show my appreciation ...

And most of all, I can't wait to build a home, a life and a future with you ...

Always and forever, my love.

Standing Alone Doesn't Mean I Am Alone. It Means I Am Strong Enough to Handle Things by Myself

I know I'm not always the easiest person to understand or get to know ...
And maybe that's just because I've been doing this life by myself for far too long ...
Maybe building high walls and keeping my guard up is part of the reason I've made it this far.
Sure, I have loving friends who are in my corner, cheering me on, and I trust them completely.
But to get to know me, to win my love, earn my trust?
That's not easy for a reason.
I used to readily let people in, and they walked away, taking bits of my heart with them as they left.
When you keep getting burned, sooner or later, you stop jumping into the fire.
I've learned to stand on my own, depend on myself and fight my own battles.
Others might call it tough, strong or independent, I just call it my life.

I don't ask for approval, and I don't seek attention.

I've learned to control what I can and let the rest happen as it's meant to.

I've proven to myself that I can take whatever life wants to throw at me ... time and again.

So, before you label me distant, cold or stubborn, take the time to get to know me.

Maybe I haven't had the easiest life, but I'm worth the effort.

I'm not everyone's cup of tea, but the ones who seek the truth beneath my tough exterior always seem to love and appreciate who I am.

So, forget what you think you know about an independent woman and maybe realize that you'll never know what I've had to endure to be standing in front of you today, smiling, strong and confident.

You don't know the price I've paid, the sacrifices I made or the failures that changed me.

You'll never know the roads I've traveled or the pain I've felt, but maybe if you're lucky, you'll feel the intensity of my passion ...

I love fiercely and I put it all out there – once you feel my fire, you'll realize who I am and how I love.

It's true, it's real and most of all, just like me,
It's completely unforgettable.
So, maybe I'm hard to understand, tough to get to know and even more challenging to love, but once you win my heart and affection, there's nothing I won't do for you.
And every day, in every way, I make my fiery love and intense passion completely worth the time it took to get past my walls.
Just like me …
Strong, loving and worth it all.

Sometimes the Hardest Part of Waking up in the Morning Is Remembering What You Were Trying to Forget Last Night

I woke up, hoping to feel refreshed after a night spent tossing and turning.

It was one of those long nights when I couldn't turn off my thoughts and my memories wouldn't give me a moment's peace.

So, as I opened my eyes, I mustered every bit of optimism about the start of a beautiful day ... Until my heart whispered the lingering thoughts I had wanted to forget.

You. Us.

The pain of our split was all too real and felt like just yesterday, though it had actually been a couple weeks already.

I knew that no matter what I told myself or what I wanted, my heart wasn't ready to let you go ... Even though my head kept telling me to move on.

That's one of the hardest places to be – when your head is at war with your heart.

Deep down, I knew what was best for me and what I needed to do, but there was no convincing my heart of that reality.

My emotions weren't there yet, so I was stuck, all the time, between a mind trying to forget and a heart that wouldn't let me.

It was a constant montage at night, playing a never-ending stream of us ... good, bad and ugly ... but always us.

I did the best I could and just fought for a few hours' sleep, if that, in between the nonstop thinking.

Though, as I sipped my coffee that morning, I noticed that everything hurt just a little less and the sunlight was a little bit brighter.

Maybe, I thought, this is how it happens.

The more time passes, the less you feel, the less you hurt, the less you remember ...

Until one day, it's all just a distant memory.

I couldn't help but smile at the possibility of relief.

I knew I'd have to make peace with the past before I could ever really move on, but suddenly, I felt a twinge that I didn't have before.

Maybe it wasn't a bold epiphany and maybe it didn't make anything better instantly ... but now, I finally realized that I could do this.

Things would get better; the pain would begin to subside; I'd start to find my way again.

That, for now, would have to be enough.

After all, now, I had something I didn't have last night, and it changed everything ...

Something that had been eluding me for far too long: Hope.

And I decided to keep building on that ... all the way to my newfound happiness.

It might take a while, but I finally knew that I could make my way away from the pain of us.

Step by step and day by day, I'd start to love myself again ...

And finally, be able to let you go.

Don't Apologize for Your Fire. Own It

I used to worry about what everyone thought of me, and I fretted if I didn't fit into what they thought I should be.
I spent my time chasing the images and labels the world tried to fit me into until one day, I had finally had enough of the nonsense.
I realized that the happiness I was chasing wasn't my own – it was everyone else's – and I made up my mind that my happiness was more important than that.
I couldn't please everyone and myself at the same time, so I made a choice ...
I chose myself.
And it was the best decision I've ever made.
I stopped apologizing for who I was and started loving the parts about me that the world wanted to change.
I'll never be happy squeezing into some box or label about what I "should be."
Sure, I'm a mess some days and other times, I don't know whether I'm coming or going, but I live every moment authentically.
No games, fake pretenses or pretending ...
With me, what you see is what you get –
Real, authentic and genuine.

I may not sugarcoat, play nice or say what you want to hear, but I'll always tell you the truth ...
The world needs more of that.
I'm a handful to most, they'd say, but I'm a handful of the best things:
Passion, determination, courage and, of course, my signature feisty attitude.
So, forgive me if I don't ask anyone's permission to live my life the way I see fit or if I don't apologize for being true to myself.
I will not seek approval for my life, now or ever.
I'm too fiery for some, too sassy for others, and that's okay ...
I know I'm not everyone's favorite person.
I'm good to my people – the ones who get me.
They accept and appreciate everything about me – even when I'm ugly crying about a bad decision or because I chased the wrong love.
No judgment, just love.
That's how I know they're my people because they treat me like I treat them.
I'm not saying that I've got it all together, because I don't, not even close.
I still cry in the shower sometimes and lay in bed mustering up the strength to just get up and face the day.

All in all, most days I'm a beautiful mess and a handful of disaster, but I'll always have a smile on my face and a pep in my step.

Not for anyone but me, because I'm living my life the best I can, taking each day one at a time and making the most of the moments that give me happiness.

Maybe I'd like more of them and maybe each day doesn't go exactly the way I planned, but I acknowledge the gifts I have and the people I'm blessed with.

I'm real, I'm down to earth and I'm passionate about the things and people I care about.

The day I stopped chasing the wrong things and started being the real me, everything changed.

Now, maybe every day isn't beautiful, but there's beauty in every day ...

Starting with me.

And no one can ever take that away from me. Beautiful, strong and free.

For Those Who See My Greatness Within, Even When I Don't See It in Myself

I'm sending love to all my people out there –
my loved ones, my tribe, my friends that
became family.
All the ones who are there for me when I need
them, without judgement, criticism or
disapproval.
They love me unconditionally when I need it
most, and they celebrate me when I'm at my
best.
I call them a lot of things: my besties, my BFFs,
my ride or dies, my best friends, my hearts.
They wipe away my ugly tears when I've had
my heart broken for the millionth time, and they
hold my hand when I'm facing the storms of
uncertainty.
No matter how long it's been since we talked or
whatever we need, we can pick up right where
we left off.
That's what makes us special: we have an
unbreakable bond that time, disagreement or
trouble can't break.
We've got each other's backs, regardless of
what's happening.

We share our hopes, dreams, fears and problems; that's just who we are and what we do.

I know that no matter what time of the day or night, I can call them, and they'll pick up.

They may not be so fond of the middle of the night calls, but they'd never admit it.

It's okay – I know I make them want to kill me sometimes as I make all the wrong decisions and choose all the wrong loves – even when they tell me not to.

Through all the tears, the laughter and the moments we've shared all this time, I'm proud to call them my friends.

Brothers from another mother and sisters from other misters, even the family that became even closer, I'm blessed to have them in my corner.

Friends are the family we choose, and I choose them every day in every way.

There really aren't words to describe how very much I love my people and what they mean to me.

They've always been there, every step of the way ...

Believing in me when I didn't believe in myself ... and that's pretty often.

So, thank you for standing beside me through it all, loving me when I'm at my worst and celebrating me at my best.

No matter what happens tomorrow or the challenges we face, I know that we can overcome it all, hand in hand and heart to heart.

That's who we are and how strong we will always be.

So, when I look out over my life, I take a deep breath and smile.

Life's pretty amazing when you're surrounded by the people that love you ...

So, to all my friends, thank you for being you and always being there.

You have always made everything in my life just that much better, and without you, life wouldn't be the same.

You will always be people, and I love you more than you'll ever know.

Thank you.

Everything She's Not Saying

She often gets to a place where she's out of words, out of patience, out of all the things that make her speak her mind.

When she finds herself there, she knows it's a tenuous place to be.

After all, it's not what she says when she's upset, fiery or passionate that truly defines her ... It's those moments of silence, when she has run out of words that will tell you everything you need to know.

Whether she's too tired, doesn't care or just can't muster up the energy to talk anymore ... those are the times when – if you pay close enough attention – you'll truly begin to understand her.

Her eyes will reveal things about her soul that words can never tell you: her deepest meanings and secrets lie beyond the windows that guard her truths.

Many people who have crossed her path never truly understood her, because they didn't pay attention to the things she didn't say, the messages from her heart and soul that she protects from the world.

The most beautiful creatures are the ones that have been hurt the deepest, fought for who they've become and loved the hardest.

She's not the easiest mystery to unravel nor the easiest person to understand, but once you've dived deeper into her depths and begun to witness her innermost places ...

You'll soon begin to understand why she's a treasure that is without measure.

She protects her heart with fierce courage because she refuses to allow anyone to disrespect her, easily hurt her or waste her time anymore.

She's protective of her people and passionate about what she believes in.

Her deepest and most intense truths are the words that she doesn't speak and the things she doesn't allow just anyone to know about her.

So, when you meet a woman like her, take your time and immerse yourself in one of the deepest, most beautiful people you'll ever meet ... A strong and fiercely independent woman.

Don't miss the chance to fully comprehend all that she is ...

Starting with the things she isn't saying.

Look beyond her words into her eyes, and you'll discover the true beauty of a woman lies deep within.

Soulfully in Sync

I want more than superficial love ...
I need the deep, soulful connection that makes
my heart sigh.
I've had ordinary desire and temporary longing;
I'm done settling for those skin-deep feelings.
If it doesn't stir my soul, enflame my heart and
fill my spirit with butterflies, then that's not my
kind of love.
Don't get me wrong, I still want animal
attraction, passionate fire and intimate
closeness ... but I don't want just that ...
I need so much more than simple pleasures.
I crave it all ... and I will accept nothing less.
Let's do all the things that stimulate our mental
connection – lie in bed reading to each other,
have deep talks for hours about everything and
nothing, lose ourselves in each other's minds
deeply and intimately.
Maybe I'm a dreamer and holding out for the
impossible, but it's what I want and deserve.
Let's set the night on fire with the chain
reaction of our love story – from the mind to the
soul to everything else – that transcends the
normalcy of the ordinary.

Stimulate my mind, connect with my soul, set my heart on fire so that even the smallest touch electrifies our skin.

I've waited a lifetime to find this sort of love, and until you found me, I didn't know what all that meant ... it was all just wishes and wants. You've made it more than real; you've transformed my life into the love story I had long dreamt of.

I always knew what I wanted in life and love, but you came into my world and made it all real.

You've made your heart into my home, your arms where I belong and the future beautiful by your side.

Everything's better when it's shared with someone you love.

Thank you for making all the dead ends and broken roads worth every wrong turn and bad decision.

I couldn't have dreamt that I would find everything I had ever wanted in you.

In the middle of an ordinary life, you gave me a fairytale.

Maybe You're Actually on a Shortcut to a Better Path

She'd often cry herself to sleep, feeling utterly lost and alone as she sought purpose in a life that seemed to escape her, no matter how hard she looked.

She'd made the mistake of thinking love could fill that void, and that led to her repeated heartache from trying to turn projects into partners.

She tried to find herself through others, and it never worked out and it never could.

She sobbed so often about the broken roads and burned bridges, asking why things didn't ever seem to work out ...

She didn't understand why it was so hard to be happy ... when that's all she really wanted.

She would stare so long at the closed doors lamenting the losses and the new chances that passed her by.

Dwelling in darkness is a tough place to be when you're not really sure how to look for the light ...

But, in the midst of her sorrow – and while she thought herself lost – a simple thought from her dearest friend catapulted her thinking into a new direction altogether ...

"Perhaps you've never been lost at all. Maybe you were led from the places you were never meant to be so that you could find your way to a better path."

She was stunned.

She'd never really trusted her life to lead her where she was meant to be.

She had been too busy trying to turn frogs into princes and to make square pegs fit into round holes ...

And she found herself laughing.

"No wonder it never worked out the way I wanted ... I never needed the things I lost along the way."

She realized that she had always been led to something better each time, though she had not recognized that at the time.

She had slowly begun to appreciate who she was as her attempts to find love failed disastrously.

That was it. How could she love another until she found her way back to herself?

She couldn't.

She wouldn't.

So, she dug deeply and began to find her happiness somewhere she'd never thought to look for it: within herself.

Day by day, step by step, she slowly and painfully began to understand who she was and to find the answers she had always looked for in other people.

It was hard being alone; she had never done that before, not in all her life.

It was scary even, but she kept going, and she found that it became beautiful ... through the darkness and the rain, she discovered that the other side of her struggle was more amazing than she'd ever thought possible.

It's funny how life works sometimes.

Then, on a bright spring day, she turned a corner and ran right into a young man.

They both collapsed in shock and laughter. That moment, frozen in time (as she often looked back in fondness), was the instant she realized why it never worked out with anyone else before.

In his eyes, she immediately recognized why the broken roads had led her straight to him, and she felt both stunned and blessed.

She knew then that every wrong turn had helped her find her way home to herself ...

And right where she was meant to be:
Happy, at long last.

I See You, You Are Enough, and You Are Not Alone

I know that sometimes, when the world weighs heavily on your shoulders, you feel utterly alone and lost.

I realize that there are many days you wonder if anything you do matters.

Whatever you've been feeling, whatever you've been thinking, however you've been hurting ... I'm here to tell you that you are not alone.

There are so many of us walking the same path, with the same struggles, asking the same questions.

Take heart, Darling, for we will keep walking beside you, hand in hand and heart to heart.

And sometimes, just knowing someone is there can be the spark you need to get back up again.

I know that you try, you fight, and you love with such an amazing heart ... and you wonder why you don't get the same in return.

You will – perhaps not immediately, but the love you put out in the world always comes back to you tenfold.

I know you've had a hard past and there are days you don't want to keep going, but I'm telling you, don't quit.

The world needs amazing people like you ... you're a light when you don't even realize it.

Your life may not feel great, and you may question why you even try, but you've been down before, and you found a way then – You can find a way now.

Maybe you've stopped believing in yourself, and I get that ...

I've been right where you are before.

Telling myself that I didn't have anyone and that no one cared, feeling sorry for myself because nothing ever seemed to work out.

Life, love, happiness ... I always ended up back at the same place: disconsolate and distraught.

But I'm here to tell you that you've got a choice.

You can stay in the darkness, learn to love rock bottom, or you can choose to fight back. Take back your life, claw out of the pits and pull yourself out of the misery.

If you can't believe in and love yourself first, how can you expect anyone else to?

We both know you can do this – you can do anything you set your mind to.

Stop feeling sorry for yourself and start taking baby steps forward.

That last love that broke you or the past that's weighing you down?

Let it go. It's not helping you find your way or grow.

You'll be amazed at how much easier it is to push forward when you're not carrying the pain of yesterday.

I won't tell you it will be easy, fast or painless, because chances are, it will be none of those things ... but it will be worth everything.

Maybe you'll tell me you can't, that you weren't meant to rise from the ashes or that you're too tired and old.

Stop and remember who you used to be and the dreams you had.

They're right where you left them, just waiting to be found again ...

Just like you.

You've been gone so long, maybe it's time to come home and remember who you truly are.

But it's all a choice.

Your choice.

I'm telling you that you're not alone, that you're worth it and you can do this.

If you don't believe, take some of my belief in you ... I have enough for both of us.

You can never write a new beginning, but you can always turn the page and begin to write new chapters.

Here's the pen.

It's time to rewrite who you are, where you're going and what you can do.

I believe in you.

Don't Worry About Being Beautiful, Be Authentic

I used to spend my days trying to be what I thought would make everyone else happy and help me fit in.

Truth is, nothing of that ever made me happy or helped me feel good about myself.

They told me to be pretty, be this or be that.

I realized then they didn't care who or what I was, they just wanted me to help them feel better about themselves by making me fit into their little boxes and labels ...

It made them feel in control, and they thought it helped them understand me ...

But that wasn't my truth.

And I'm done playing by their rules. I'm done trying to become something I was never meant to be.

I don't care about being labeled, understood or fitting in.

What matters to me is being true to myself, and I'll never be able to do that chasing their dreams.

Beautiful? Pretty? Trendy?

Those are words that don't matter to me because they're not real.

What's real is who I am and the things about me that are awesome.

Intelligent, witty, authentic, fun ... the list goes on and on, because I'm a unique person blessed with original qualities.

Please don't try to describe me with a generic word meant to box me in or make me seem like everyone else ...

Because I'm far from it.

Call me quirky, outrageous and all those fun words that mean I make some people uncomfortable.

I can't help but laugh at the thought of it.

I know they don't understand why I choose to be the way that I am, and they don't have to.

I like who I am, and I like my life ...

From my weird friends – who I adore for their weirdness – to the love I share to the adventures I chase ...

It's all a reflection of me, and I like who I'm becoming.

Maybe I won't win an award for being "the best of everyone just like me," but I'll be happy, original and one of a kind.

Having a content soul and full heart matters much more to me than impressing people I don't care about in ways that don't matter for attention I don't want.

So, save the simple, superficial words to describe someone else – maybe someone who thinks those words are wonderful.

I'll stick to being who I am and wholly indescribable.

Because at the end of the day, those words can never even get close to the awesomeness that is me.

An Old Soul

She couldn't tell you exactly why she always felt different, only that she did.

People would always tell her that she was wise beyond her years, but she thought that was just their way of being nice.

But the more time that passed, the more she realized that she possessed an uncommon wisdom, a thirst for knowledge and an understanding that she didn't know how she'd come to possess.

Things that others missed, she'd totally comprehend in a way that stumped even her.

Many thought she was a little odd or perhaps eccentric, but that was just her soul shining through.

It made some uncomfortable, her depth and relative understanding, but the people that got her – truly got her – loved her intensely and infinitely.

Perhaps they appreciated her uniqueness, perhaps they had old souls themselves … all she knew was that she loved her close circle, and they were always there for her.

The things that others didn't see, feel or notice – the wisdom, the energies, the truths behind so many things in life – were so very obvious to her.

But she realized that was part of her gift – and curse – of knowing without knowing why.

She learned to harness her gifts and make peace with herself, and she sought all the ways she could become much more content.

Her soul, full of vibrant energy and loving wonder, defined who she was and brought her a sense of peace that she couldn't always describe.

She always seemed to find her way, and she began to love the process of finding herself.

Every flaw, mistake and depth that she uncovered made her appreciate the person she was becoming.

Most of all, she found peace in knowing that having an old soul could set you free ...

And with that newfound courage, she unfurled her wings and began to fly ...

Amazing, strong and free.

Our Souls Are the Same

From the very first moment, we knew.
We'd both heard all the stories and knew all
the ways love was supposed to feel, but until
you come face to face with that indescribable
moment when you just know that they're the
one, it's all just pretty words.
But in that magical moment when you know,
everything changes ... your hopes, dreams and
even where you want to be.
All I could think of was you ... being beside
you, in your arms, holding you close, building a
future together.
It's almost unbelievable when you find yourself
saying the same things at the same times,
liking the same weird things or just sharing a
powerful connection that can't be denied.
I'd always heard others talking about that
intimate closeness that two people can share,
but like most, I brushed it off as fairytale
nonsense.
And then I met you.
You changed everything I thought I knew about
love, and I've never been so happy to be
utterly wrong.

We're the same, you and I, and always have been.

In all the big, beautiful ways and even the little gorgeous ways too.

Where I stop and you start, I'll never know – nor do I want to.

There are a lot of things I don't know about this life, but I do know this:

You've been mine since before we ever met, even when you were just a dream.

Since you found me, everything has changed, and I never want to go back to the way things used to be.

With you is where I belong.

In my arms, in my heart and forever in love.

I Would Rather Be Alone Than Have a Love That Is Lonely

I tried ... I really did.

I poured everything I had into us, in every way I knew how to try and keep our love alive.

What I learned the hard way is that it takes two people to make a relationship truly work.

I won't blame you for your choices because you did what made you happy – and obviously, my happiness wasn't part of that agenda.

I gave you everything and asked for so little in return, but that was my first mistake.

I sacrificed, gave and loved all that I could, and I should have demanded more.

I deserve more.

By lowering my expectations, I lost self-respect and started losing myself, too.

It's a lonely feeling to be in a relationship and not have anyone you can talk to or confide in ... But that's where we've ended up, and I'm done settling for less than what I'm worth.

It's no one's fault but my own for allowing things to end up in this place.

Maybe if I'd stood up for what I wanted and truly needed, things might have been different ... I'll probably never know.

What I do know is that walking away now with some shred of my dignity and self-respect means more than waiting around on someone who doesn't really seem to care.

I've told you all this time and again, and like always, you'd brush me off and tell me I was being needy ...

And yes, I did need you to step up and show me that you loved me, not just say the words you thought I wanted to hear with no action to back them up.

I never thought love could make me feel empty, alone and isolated, but that's just where I am.

Really, though, it's not love making me feel that way – it's the lack of love.

So, as I leave my key and a note on the table, know that I'll always care about you, but sometimes, that's just not enough.

I'm doing what I need to do to be happy again, and if you care even a little, you'll let me go in peace to find my way.

After all, I know I'll be better off on my own than having an empty and lonely love story ... because we both know that's not really a love story, it's just a story.

But thanks to you, I know everything I don't want in another person or a relationship.
I'm taking this time for me now, and it's long overdue.
Love isn't going anywhere, and I'm done trying to turn projects into partners.
I'm choosing the love story where I know I'll get what I give ...
I'm loving myself first now.
And there's nothing wrong with that if you ask me.
One step at a time, finding my way back to the light.
I can do this.

I've Outgrown My Old Story, I'm Ready for a New Adventure

I woke up this morning and realized that I need more ...

More of the things that fill my soul and less of the things that stress me out.

I've been living day to day for so long that I don't even think I know how to live any differently ... but I'm going to try.

I'm done with the old stuff – the parts of my life that weigh me down, hurt me and make me unhappy.

Today, I've chosen to start writing a new chapter ... something so new and different that it will feel strange for a while, until it doesn't anymore.

I've been down lately, but I'm not going to stay down anymore.

I'm turning my setbacks into a comeback, and I'm turning the page to start searching for my bliss.

Maybe it'll take a while because I don't know where I'm going.

Maybe it'll be a little awkward and humbling because I won't always know what I'm doing.

Maybe it'll be painful because the best kinds of growth usually are.

I've decided to leave behind the people, the places and the things that don't contribute to my happiness.

I've learned the hard way that not everyone wants you to be happy.

Some people can be selfish, and if it doesn't fit into their agenda then they won't support you. No more.

I'm surrounding myself with the people who love and accept me for who I am.

And if there's not enough of them, then I'm stepping outside my comfort zone and making new friends and broadening my horizons.

I can't live or love small anymore – I've tried that, and I'll never be happy with that.

I wear my heart on my sleeve and I love my people with everything I have ... and that's just what I'm going to keep doing.

Maybe I get hurt more than most, maybe I choose the wrong people to love sometimes, but I will never stop listening to my heart.

So, as I step out into a new day, I'm forging a new mindset and a new courage.

While I may never be the kind of brave that scales mountains or jumps out of planes, I can be brave in all the little ways that matter every day ...

Being kind to strangers, paying compliments, helping people in need, and chasing my own adventure.

That's part of my new story, and I'm both excited and wonderfully scared to start living it.

A new day, a new chapter and a new me.

Strong, beautiful and brave.

I Am Not What Happened to Me, I Am What I Choose to Become

I fought for so long to simply survive my life, trying to get by day to day.
I'd get up most days wondering how I'd make it, mustering up my courage and strength to keep going.
I got knocked down, dragged around and left to fail, time and again.
The world didn't give me a chance and, frankly, I don't know that I did, either.
But when you're stuck at the bottom and trying not to suffocate, you make a choice:
Either give up and accept failure or you dig deep, find something brave in yourself and rise up again.
Truth is, my life and my story never gave me a choice ...
There were too many people and there was too much to lose to just give up ...
So, I did the only thing I knew to do.
I braved the flames of my struggles, and they lit my soul on fire.
You learn a lot about yourself when you're alone at rock bottom, fighting for survival, trying to find the strength to keep going.

I did.

I chose not to be defined by what happened to me or by where I've been.

I forgave the people along the way that hurt me, and I started to let go of the pain that I had let shackle me ...

That's not who I am.

For too long, I had let past pain dictate my life. Not anymore.

I'm accepting responsibility for the choices I've made and where I've been.

I'm making peace with my past so that I can build a better future, piece by piece.

It's not easy – I still have days when the memories haunt me, and the pain comes back to visit.

But I do what I have to do, and I push through those times.

I still have days when I cry in the shower, and I have times where just getting out of bed takes everything I have.

Maybe that's just part of the journey.

My days won't all be great, and they can't all be bad, I get that now.

I find the small victories in the hard days, and I appreciate the good times.

But most of all, I never forget where I've been and the people who helped me forge my strength along the way.

I'm not a victim, a survivor or broken.

I'm a fighter, I'm a warrior, and I'm strong.

Because I choose to be.

Maybe it's not always pretty or easy, but I'm going to own my experiences and keep striving to be a better person, every day in every way.

I look back and wonder how I kept going sometimes, but then I realize I had to go through the hardships to get stronger, wiser and better.

Because of everything, I can smile now and know, no matter what:

I got this.

You Will Forever Be My Always

You asked me how I knew that I loved you.
You wondered why I chose you.
Honestly?
I didn't choose you.
My heart fell in love with yours.
Our souls connected in a way I'd never known.
I saw it in your eyes, felt it in your touch.
Butterflies made room for physical cravings –
to hold you, to be close to you.
When I was away from you, every fiber of my
being longed to be in your arms again.
Those feelings – emotional, physical and
soulful – redefined everything I ever thought I
knew about love.
You were the missing piece, the safe place, the
beautiful truth I had always searched for.
In that moment, when your lips touched mine
for the very first time, it was more than a
feeling or an emotion.
It was meant to be.
When I kissed your lips and realized how
wrong every other kiss had ever been, it was
then that I more than knew.

The answer that I had long sought showed up
just when it was meant to, not a moment
sooner.

I look in your beautiful eyes and see the
reflections of my soul, and I know all the
reasons why I fell for you.

And I'll spend the rest of my days reminding
you of all the ways you're beloved to me.

My love for you can't be described in any
words I've ever known,

And I can't verbalize forever in a way that
doesn't pale in comparison to the beautiful love
that I found in you.

I love you, for you will forever be my always.

She never really set out to become the person she was.

Her life and her story never gave her any other choice.

Most people who knew her didn't really think she could make it: she wasn't born with a silver spoon, and no one ever gave her anything, including a chance.

She didn't have extravagant dreams.

In fact, she simply wanted the same things that most people did – it just so happened that the road she had to travel was harder and longer than most would ever know.

She fought to keep a positive attitude, but there were just those times when everything in her wanted to give up.

She often didn't see the point of struggling – barely surviving – and then repeating that day in and day out.

She wanted more than to just exist, she wanted the chance to live ... whatever that took, she was willing to risk it.

You see, miracles and luck are so often the products of hard work.

And sometimes, changes are so gradual that you can't even really see them at first.

So, she didn't think about it as she kept pushing forward and fighting for her happiness. And eventually the hard days began to grow a little easier and the things that used to weigh her down began to feel a little lighter.

Her strength grew and so did her joy.

She hadn't set out to be strong, but she had much more to do in her life and she would need every iota of strength, bravery and courage to persevere.

Even through the times that brought her to her knees. Even through the times that broke her. But the bitter sweetly beautiful thing that also happened?

She got up, dusted herself off and started to put herself back together again each and every time.

If not for the hard roads she'd traveled, she'd never have had what she needed to fight through the trials of her life and keep going.

Her struggles had transformed her into a strong and independent woman.

Looking back, she'd never change where she'd been, because she knew that's what it took to make her the person she became.

On the way to an extraordinary life, she became all the things she never thought she could ...

A strong woman.

A warrior.

A believer ...

Most of all, a Phoenix rising ...

And her time was now.

Through the ashes and fires that had once consumed her,

She finally became strong enough to choose ...

To become whoever she wanted to be.

There are just things in my past I won't talk about.

That doesn't mean I haven't dealt with them, made peace with them or confronted what they did to me ...

It just means I'm not giving those things that happened and the people who hurt me power over me anymore.

I know that the people, places and things will always be part of my story – lessons I had to learn and grow from to become the person I am today –

But it doesn't mean I have to hold onto the past.

I've let it go because I realized that the longer I held onto the pain, the deeper I let the pain seep into my soul ...

And I'm not going to let that happen, not anymore.

Sure, I used to have a hard time letting go of people who chose to walk away, but that baggage became heavier and heavier until I couldn't carry it anymore.

It was a painful process that caused many tears, but amazingly, the more I began to let go, the lighter my burdens started to feel.
So, please understand that if I don't want to talk about something I've been through, it's not because I'm denying that it happened or regretting where I've been.
All those things will always be a part of me.
I just don't want to rehash and relive the trauma of things that make me feel bad.
Healing is a lifelong process, and day by day I'm on my way to a healthier me.
So, let's talk about today, tomorrow and the blessings we have.
The future we can build together is more important to me than talking about something I went through a long time ago.
I'm done looking over my shoulder at what has been. I'm living for today, tomorrow and where we're headed.
So, take my hand – let's walk and talk for a while.
About life, us, our dreams and whatever comes to mind ...
Let's leave what has been where it belongs – in the past – and move on.

We have much more beautiful things to explore ... And I can't wait to spend hours doing exactly that.

That sounds pretty amazing if you ask me.

Actually, how about a road trip to nowhere and everywhere?

There's magic all around us ... let's start making our own, one day, one hope and one dream at a time.

What You Can When You Can

Stop and take a breath.
Life can be overwhelming, I know.
All the things to do, every day, and never
enough time to do them in ...
And especially, no time for yourself.
It's okay not to be okay, it's okay not to get it all
done, it's okay to take a break, it's okay to ask
for help.
You're doing all you can with what you have ...
and that's enough.
You're enough – in fact, you're way more than
enough.
You're not a failure if you don't get it all done in
a day or if you make mistakes.
We're all human, we all stumble and fall; we all
need time to rest.
Take that time.
Sit, drink some coffee and read.
Kick back outside and take in the beauty of
nature.
Veg out on the couch and watch a TV show.
If you're running yourself empty, you'll have
nothing left to give to the people in your life
who need you ...
Most of all, yourself.

Stop trying to be perfect, stop competing with what everyone else is doing, stop trying to get everything done in a day.

Be kind to yourself.

Listen to your body when it needs rest and give yourself what you need.

Don't get so busy trying to do that you forget to live.

Pause for a bit.

Live in the moment, appreciate the good in your life, enjoy the little things.

You think you'll look back and remember the big things, but you'll find that it's the little things that will make you smile.

The laughter of a friend.

The hug of a loved one.

A quiet meal with someone special.

Don't let those chances to make memories slip through your fingers.

It's not about changing the world, maybe just try changing your world ...

A healthier, happier you will spread more love and kindness than a tired, exhausted you will ever be able to.

Give yourself permission to rest.

Allow yourself to cry.

Tell yourself it's okay to not be okay.

There are no rules to life – make them as you
go.
Every day is a new chance to turn the page
and start a new chapter.
I'm handing you the pen.
It's all in your hands ...
What will be your newest and best chapter yet
be called?

I know you think I should feel bad for what's happened between us, but I didn't cause this, nor did I ever want it to come to this.
I let you dictate the terms of our relationship for far too long, and I'm done marching to your beat.
I have an opinion, a voice, and I matter too.
It's not always about you and what you want.
I don't know where along the way our relationship stopped being about us and became about you, but I'm done with that.
I'm standing up for who I am, what I want and the kind of relationship I deserve.
If you want a gal to hide behind you, beg for your attention and accept secondary treatment, then I'm not that person.
I've tried swallowing my pride and putting my needs behind yours, thinking that would make things better and that, somehow, I'd be happier ... But I became more miserable.
So, if you can't step up, be the man I need and treat me the way I deserve, that's your choice ... But I'm not sticking around for act two. I need action, not more temporary promises.

I'm not going to apologize for how I feel, and you don't get to tell me what to think or believe. I'm not a puppet and that's not a real relationship.

So, I'm opening my heart and telling you what I need ...

You can choose to either work with me to make us better, or you can keep doing whatever you want and watch me walk away. It's not that I don't love you, it's not that I don't want this, I just love myself more than to allow myself to be disrespected anymore.

So, I'm holding out my hand and asking you to meet me halfway ...

Just don't ask me to change my mind, chase you or be okay being just an option.

And most of all, don't ask me to apologize for how I feel.

Can you handle my truth?

The Heart Knows When the Search Is Over

All her life, she had searched the world over,
Longing for love and hoping to find her happily
ever after.
She turned over every stone, kissed every frog,
Looked around each corner ... to no avail.

Possibly slowly turned into never,
All the hopes she once had seemed
To vanish with bad choices and even worse
men.
She fretted as she wondered if "he" truly
existed.
She started to think fairytales didn't come true.

It was on a beautiful Sunday afternoon,
Out of nowhere and in a way completely
Unexpected, unbelievable and unanticipated,
She came face to face with a man who
seemed ... familiar.

His gaze met hers, their souls found one
another,
And in an instant, she experienced a calm
never before known.
His voice soothed her spirit,

His touch felt like home.

All the doubts and insecurities melted away,
As if they had never even existed.
Her "nevers" transformed into "always"
Her "not nows" changed into "forever."

She learned the hardest lesson of all:
Love comes in its own time and own way.
You can't predict it or even understand it.
All you can do is cherish it when it arrives.

For when Cupid's arrow finds your heart,
You'll recognize in an instant that they are the
one ...
Your true love, your soulmate, your forever
twin flame.
She smiled – she had finally kissed her last
frog.
In the middle of an ordinary life, she had found
a fairytale.

A Woman Determined to Rise

She didn't know she ended up at rock bottom,
cast aside, left for dead and forgotten.
It hurt worse than anything she'd ever known –
and she'd been through some hard times.
All her life, she was kicked around, pushed
aside, disrespected and disregarded.
When you get treated so badly and told you're
worthless for so long, you start to believe it.
But this last man, someone who promised her
that he'd be there forever, crushed her soul
with his hateful words.
He swept her away with delusions of grandeur
and then cast her aside just as quickly ...
It's one thing to break someone's heart, it's
quite another to tread on it ruthlessly.
He left her crying and feeling less than
worthless as he moved on effortlessly.
One look at her would tell you that she was a
broken woman – she had nothing left, her heart
and soul pulverized once again by lies
disguised as promises.
But as she was laying there, sobbing and
heartbroken, something snapped.

She didn't know what happened or what changed, but she felt something welling inside that she had never felt.

A small spark of courage whispered to her in her darkness.

"Get up ... rise again ... you're better than this."

Truthfully, she couldn't really tell you what happened next, but she dried her eyes, pulled her hair back and glared fiercely into the mirror.

She exhaled forcibly and a gleam slowly appeared in her eye.

Her voice cracked as she spoke words she'd never forget.

"Never again."

Never again would she allow anyone to disrespect and mistreat her.

Never again would she settle for less than she deserved.

Never again would she stay down.

She knew it would be the hardest thing she'd ever done ... but then, after you've got nothing to lose, there's nowhere to go but up.

She pulled herself up and made a promise to herself that she intended to keep.

"No matter how hard, how long or how painful this may be, I'm going to rise from the ashes and become the fire that once burned me down."

No more excuses and no more apologies.
Just her and a fierce determination to fight, claw and battle her way back.
She was done asking for permission and determined to forget the pity party.
She didn't know where she was going or how she'd get there, but anywhere was better than where she was ...
Day by day and step by step, she'd forge a new path out of the pain and into the light ...
Afterall, there is no force equal to the strength of a woman determined to rise.

Just a Chapter, Not the Whole Story

You may have opened your eyes this morning
and felt like the world is stacked against you.
You've had a tough time lately, I know.
But I'm here to tell you that this isn't your whole
story, it's just a chapter.
Maybe it's gone on longer than you've wanted,
been hard to endure and left you feeling down.
But chin up, Darling.
It's always darkest before dawn and it won't
rain forever – you've just got to hold onto what
you believe in, dig deeply and find your
courage.
Maybe you've lost your way, forgotten your
voice and can't find your happiness like you
used to be able to,
But this too shall pass.
Whether it's been life knocking you down, a
relationship falling apart or just feeling low, I'm
telling you that you got this.
Take my hand and let's walk a while.
Let's talk about who you are and what amazing
things you're capable of ... because you are
unstoppable when you choose to be.

Bravery isn't about turning it around immediately; it's about getting up every single day and doing the best you can.

It's okay to not be okay.

It's okay to need rest or ask for help.

It's okay to fall and get knocked down ...

Just choose to keep getting back up, keep fighting, keep holding your head high.

What you've been through doesn't define you, and you're more than you give yourself credit for ... though you may feel alone and helpless right now, you are powerful, and it's up to you to claw your way out or sink deeper into the darkness.

And I'm right here to remind you that you're all the things you've stopped believing in about yourself ...

You are strong.

You are more than enough.

You are capable of rising again.

Maybe it won't be easy, maybe it will hurt some.

But I promise you that you can do it.

Start with a step.

Start by knowing that you can find your wings if only you look for them.

Stop caging yourself and start breaking free.

Turn the page.

Start a new chapter.

Most of all, just start to believe.

You've always had the power inside of yourself

... Now it's time to use it.

You got this, Darling ...

Now and always.

Believe.

I Just Need Someone Who Won't Give Up When Loving Me Gets Hard

I know there are times when I'm pretty hard to love – almost impossible, it seems.
I don't mean to be difficult or make our relationship challenging, I just have days that are hard for me.
Maybe my hair won't act right, maybe I didn't sleep well last night, maybe I woke up in a mood.
I don't really know why I'm a handful some days; it's never my intention.
It's probably the same reason why I cry suddenly and can get frustrated at the smallest things.
I really couldn't tell you.
But I do know this:
I appreciate you never turning your back on me when I'm being hard to love.
I know you lose patience with me when I'm being unreasonable, but I'm so grateful that you keep loving me when I feel most unlovable
... Because that's when I need it most.
I realize that most of the time I'm a beautiful mess – quite the splendid chaos – and that's just part of my charm ... or so I like to think.

I wish I could tell you why I'm like this sometimes, but I really don't know.

There aren't enough words to express how thankful I am that you don't give up when loving me gets hard.

Please always remember how big my heart is, how much I love you and how deeply I care.

I'm probably never going to be easy to handle, and I'm always going to have those days when I'm falling apart ...

But I can promise you that I'm always worth it, in spite of the storms sometimes brewing in my eyes.

With love in our hearts and hope in our spirits, there's nothing we can't handle, together ...

Even the most beautiful days have storms, and I promise there's always a rainbow on the other side ... I just may need a little patience and compassion 'til we get there.

I may be more challenging than most, but that won't ever change how much I love and appreciate you.

So, don't give up on me during those times when I'm hard to understand and harder to love.

Just hold me when I need it most, and we'll always come out smiling on the other side.

Hand in hand, I promise that together we can make it through anything.

She built walls around her heart and hid away
the most fragile parts of herself long ago.

She's been hurt, heartbroken and left so many
times, she did what she had to do to protect
herself.

She couldn't keep giving her heart away to the
ones who never truly deserved it ...

She needed more and was determined to get
it.

She'd rather be alone than be with someone
who didn't respect and appreciate all of her ...
even the most damaged and fragile parts that
she'd buried behind her highest walls.

As it was, many suitors came calling, but they
weren't willing to be patient, to put forth the
effort and truly dive deeper into who she was.

So, she continued on her path alone, resolved
to never settle, never chase and to never give
her love away to an undeserving person again.

She knew she was worth the time, patience
and compassion it would take to unravel her
layers.

They'd write her off as distant, difficult or cold,
but she knew that wasn't true.

She realized that she'd never be suitable for a weaker man, so she'd keep living her life to its fullest until the right one came along ...

She had become comfortable being alone and loving herself a long time ago.

If her person happened into her life and she fell in love, then she'd welcome them with open arms. She believed that when the time was right, he'd appear, see past the walls and scars, and love her just the way she wanted and deserved.

So, until then, she'd keep chasing her dreams, enjoying her life and making the most of the beautiful moments that she found in every day.

She wasn't waiting around for a hero, a white knight or her Prince Charming.

She was the heroine of her story, and she didn't need saving, fixing or completing.

She just wanted to be seen, understood and loved ...

For the strong and independent woman she was and would always be.

I'll Rise Up Better Every Time

Come on World, is that all you've got?
You've been trying to take me down for so
long, and still, you think you can beat me?
No chance.
I was built to go through the fire carrying the
weight of the world on my shoulders and keep
going, even stronger.
Keep coming at me and I'll keep getting up,
dusting myself off and rising again, better every
time.
Yeah, you knocked me down a time or two, but
you can't keep me down.
I'm too strong, too resilient and too tough to let
anyone or anything beat me.
You can't break me anymore; you've already
done that.
You can't shatter my heart; I've been through
that too many times.
You can't crush my dreams because I'm
chasing them harder than ever.
Maybe every day isn't a win, and every
moment isn't beautiful, but I seize my chances,
appreciate my life and love who I am ...

Sure, there are days when everything goes wrong and I can do no right, but I figure it out and push forward.

I keep showing up, standing tall and refusing to accept defeat ...

It's not in my warrior blood, I only get stronger from the storms that wash others away.

So, you're not going to bring me down anymore, World.

I've been through the worst, and I've kept going with a smile on my face.

So, yeah, I'm waking up today feeling pretty invincible,

And I welcome anything you think you can throw at me.

I know I'll stumble and I'll fall, but I'll keep getting up and fighting my way to the top.

I'm not perfect, but today, I feel unstoppable, flaws, scratches, scars and all.

I'm just a person who doesn't know how to quit, and I'll never let anyone or anything bring me down.

It took me a lot of failures, a lot of mistakes and way too many bad choices to get here, but I'm still standing ...

And I'll keep rising up and fighting on ...
Strong, beautiful and free.

Confidence Is the Courage to Be Yourself

I took a long hard look in the mirror this
morning and realized something:
I don't care anymore if anyone really likes me.
I've been tucking away and protecting parts of
myself for fear of disapproval from other people
for far too long.
I'm not going to live like that anymore.
No more toning myself down or watering down
my personality.
Not being true to myself has done nothing but
left me feeling empty inside.
I'm promising myself that, from now on, I'll be
the best version of me ... and I won't care who
has a problem with that.
My friends, my tribe, my people – they all know
and love the quirky, sometimes loud,
outspoken and thoughtful person I am.
If anyone else wants my hand in friendship or
heart in love, they'd better be prepared to
embrace all of me ... quirks, scars, flaws and
all.
After all, those are the parts of me that make
me amazing.
Sometimes, I'm a mess, sometimes I'm a
rockstar, but I'm always one of a kind.

So, I'm done seeking approval from the rest of the world and listening their opinions of who and what I should be.

This is my life, and I'm living it the way that I choose.

I've spent too long trying to be someone I was never meant to be, and I'm done with that noise.

It's going to take a lot of confidence and bravery at first to stand fully in the light without caring what everyone thinks ...

But I'll get there.

Maybe some won't like me, maybe some will, but I will be able to look myself in the mirror everyday knowing that I've shown up –

Real to my personality,

True to my values,

And brave enough to not care.

Maybe I'm weird,

Maybe I'm too sarcastic.

Maybe I'm a complete mess at times.

But what matters most to me and always will is showing up, standing up and speaking up.

The world needs more of those qualities:

Courageous and real voices to be heard and appreciated for their uniqueness.

I might not change the world or make history,
but I'll always tackle each and every day the
way I always should have.
My way.
Rain or shine, rise or fall, I can smile brightly
knowing that I'm living my life authentically.
In the end, that's what matters:
Filling my soul with happiness, chasing my
dreams and leaving my mark on the world,
One heart at a time … starting with my own.

Beautiful Girl, You Are So Much More

I know you've heard all your life how important
it is for you to look this way or act that way …
how pretty you look or how nicely you dress.
Stop yourself right there.
None of those things define you, so set aside
the feelings of trying to keep up with the
"shoulds."
Beauty is skin deep, but a beautiful heart and
soul are limitless.
There are countless beautiful faces and
attractive people out there, and if that makes
you happy, do that.
But don't let yourself be about JUST that.
Choose to be more, be deeper, be better, be
stronger.
True beauty – the kind that lasts, the sort of
glorious beauty that makes you glow – that
comes from within …
And you've always had it inside of you, just
waiting to be found.
Step out of your comfort zone and refuse to be
defined by a label, a word or everyone else's
opinion.
Be original, be outrageous, be unique.

The world is full of trendy people doing the same things trying to be pretty enough, glamorous enough and liked enough.

Truthfully, looks will fade and popularity will dissipate. What matters most will be the glow of your heart and soul.

Enrich your mind, fulfill your soul, stoke the passions of your heart and take the chance to be different.

Maybe you won't be the most popular person around, but the ones who appreciate you, they'll love every bit of your authentic love and real truths.

Embrace those flaws that you have hated for so long. It can be hard, I know, to love the things about yourself that you've been told are not good enough ...

But forget that noise and realize that each one of those scars, bruises and imperfections tells your story, and it's an amazing tale.

Celebrate that about yourself, and you'll find a kind of confidence and happiness you've never known ...

If it were easy, everyone would be doing it.

But take it from me ... you can.

Dig down deep and find that brave heart that's been waiting to catch fire.

Let go of the things that have been holding you back and decide that you're capable of becoming more.

Don't let life pass you by while you're trying to imitate everyone else in the same ways seeking the same attention.

Stop, take in the world around you, let it fill your soul and inspire you.

Love yourself, love your people, and most of all, learn to love your life.

You'll never feel whole or complete until you understand why you feel restless.

Beautiful woman, you are so much more than a pretty face or attractive body.

You are a gorgeous blend of deep feelings, instincts and soulful passion ...

Let those qualities guide you and teach you.

Once you find the courage, you'll finally know how to fly like you've always wanted to.

So, take this chance to be distinctly you and to release your soulful beauty ...

It'll be the best decision you've ever made.

May You Find All the Moments in Life That Take Your Breath Away

My wish for you is simple: it's everything that you deserve to be, feel and find in your life.
May you never doubt your beauty, your courage or your strength.
May you always feel the sunlight on your face and the wind at your back.
I hope that you discover all the moments in your life that change, enrich and deepen you, helping you learn things about yourself that you never knew.
May you always remember those small things that make you smile and celebrate the big stuff that warms your heart.
I hope that you travel to places off the beaten path, search for things you didn't know to find and lose yourself in adventures that fill your soul.
My wish for you is that you awaken every day knowing that life is out there, waiting for you – beautiful, wild and free – just like you.
I hope that you are able to sometimes cast aside the weight of the world and live in the moment ... to truly live and experience the beauty of life unfolding.

I hope that your life is filled with belly-aching laughter, spirit-filling hope and heart-filling love ... from friends, from family, from everyone you meet along the journey of life.

May you always find the time to notice the pockets of wonder that are all around you ... Glorious sunrises to spark your magic, amber-hued sunsets to inspire your dreams and all the gorgeous little joys that call out for your attention:

The amazing hug of a friend, a warm compliment from a stranger, the beautiful smile of a child.

May your days be filled with happiness and your nights be awash with dreams.

I wish all these things for you and much, much more ...

For you are a beautiful soul, capable of anything, with a bounty of love to give the world.

Most of all, I wish for you to find all the moments in this life that take your breath away, so that I can stand beside you, hand in hand, and soak in the immeasurable wonder of a life well lived.

I hope you fall in love with being truly alive ... every day.

If I Ever Become Just an Option, Don't Choose Me

When we met, you knew what kind of person I was: I was clear about my intentions.
I don't play games, nor do I tolerate players ... I leave that amusement for those chasing shallow feelings and lackluster dreams.
No, I told you that I needed more, I craved the truth, and I deserved the best.
If you're not willing to step up and have a mature relationship, then now is the time to set the record straight.
I'm not settling for being an option, and I'm never going to be your "maybe."
If you don't know what you want or if you have to stop and think, then I'm not the one for you.
I play for keeps, and I wear my heart on my sleeve – anything less than soul-stirring, heart-sparking passion doesn't interest me ...
I've kissed enough frogs to know that I'm holding out for the one who can make me feel like nothing I've ever known.
Maybe I'm a dreamer, but I want the kisses that bring forth butterflies, the touches that give me chills, and the looks that singe my soul.

I don't know if you're up to the task or if you can handle my heat, but if you're not willing to face the fire of my passion, then let's just part ways now.

I'm never going to chase you, beg for your attention or be anything less than a priority.

I realize that you may think I'm a handful, too much or demanding, but I know my worth ... that's never changing.

I'm showing you who I am, and you'll always know where you stand with me ...

So, I'm fiery, I'm strong-willed and I'm one of a kind, and if you didn't know that by now, start paying attention.

I'm not waiting around for you to figure it out, think about things or play the field. Love isn't a competition, and I'm not a prize for your possession.

I'm real, I'm authentic and you'll never meet another person like me.

Maybe you're not ready, maybe you're working things out or just don't know what you want ... and I'm good with that, everyone has their own path ...

Just don't expect me to be waiting for you at the end of the road, hoping you'll let me love you.

I've built high walls around my heart, and I
don't just let anyone in ...
But this is who I am and how I feel, take it or
leave it.
Are you stepping up to try to win my heart or
walking away?
I don't need to be fixed or saved; I just want to
be loved ... just as I am.

She Was Born Wild

She loved and lived by the measure of her
heart, and no one could tell her differently.
She refused to settle or quit even though she
knew her dreams might go up in flames …
And take her with them.
But that's just it, she didn't care.
She had hurt a thousand nights before and
would suffer the pain of a thousand more
before she gave up and stopped believing in
lasting love.
She was a dreamer, a lover and a fighter, and
she lived without apologies or regrets.
She drew inspiration from her joys and pains
…
She learned from her victories and failures …
How to want more and never settle for less
than she deserved.
She was willing to burn in the pursuit of her
passions so that she might finally find her
forever.
And the world was better for it.
We all need the dreamers, those brave souls
who believe against all odds.
Who don't let the fires of their hearts turn to
ash,

But instead breathe life into the embers.
Chase them, like she did, until you find your own happiness.
If she had to choose between risking the fire and staying safe on ice, she would choose to burn every time.
And she knew that when she finally found her heart's desire, her journey would end … but her next adventure would just be starting, for every end is also a new beginning.
Like the Phoenix rising, glorious from the ashes, her story was born of wildfire.
Better to burn for her love than to waste away in a vacuum.
She would never sell her soul for the price of love …
she'd give all of her life instead.

Never Run Back to What Broke You

She knew he was bad for her the moment she met him, but there was something irresistible in the way he talked, the way he moved ... the very way he made her feel.

She couldn't put her finger on it, but he sparked something in her she'd never felt, and it drove her wild.

But she soon found that something hot can burn you in both good ways and bad ...

And the ugly part soon reared its head.

Where once she had been his priority, she found him slipping away from her ...

Where she had felt confident in their love, she soon felt anything but.

He would never admit it – not that she could ever get him to truly talk about his feelings anyway – but she knew.

She knew what was happening and that his attention was being diverted ...

And she knew she deserved better than that.

So, when the reality of the heartbreak became apparent, all she could do was fight not to fall apart.

His loss nearly broke her ... her heart, her will, her courage.

As she turned to walk away, wiping away the tears he had so carelessly caused, her eyes met his and he motioned for her to come back. Before, she had always been willing to be there for him, always responding to his needs ... but that was before.

Looking back over her shoulder, she knew she had a choice to make.

Return to the person and situation that had shattered her into a million pieces ...

Or choose herself and keep walking.

Head down, tears streaming, she chose.

She chose herself ... she chose to be free.

She's the Worst Combination of Thinking Too Much, Feeling Too Deeply and Loving Too Hard

She wished so many times that she could turn off her heart and mind, for they tirelessly worked in overdrive.

She had this awful habit of getting too attached to the wrong person and then falling apart as her heart was continually broken time and again.

She just wanted what everyone else seemed to have – the romance that would ease her loneliness and the love to fill her heart.

But all the roads she traveled in search of those things often crumbled beneath her feet.

She would lay in bed awake at night as the feelings of loneliness and regret washed over her.

Her mind would race back to memories past, of relationships that didn't work out and loves that failed for one reason or another.

She would try to think about what went wrong or what she could have done differently ...

Never truly understanding that the failure wasn't hers to carry alone.

Perhaps she self-sabotaged sometimes and maybe she fell too hard, too fast ... but she always dove into love with pure intentions and a fierce heart ...

For loving hard was just part of who she was. She didn't believe in doing anything halfway, especially when it came to matters of the heart. Despite all the dead ends and failed chances, she never stopped believing that her happily ever after would happen.

She was relentlessly optimistic in everything she did and tried, though those long and sleepless hours would mire her thoughts in a downward spiral that she so desperately tried to escape ...

But she always stayed true to herself and never gave up on her dreams, no matter the failures or people who told her real love didn't exist anymore.

She knew better than to listen to skeptics that had never experienced the pure intimacy that was true love.

Maybe she'd find it, or it would find her, but she kept her head high and her wings flying.

You could call her foolish, naive or unrealistic, but her dreams were what kept her inspired, what helped her conquer her hardest days.

Maybe the nights were sometimes long and perhaps the feelings could be too intense, but she'd never change anything about who she was or what she believed in.

It was that belief and determination that picked her up when she fell, that inspired her when she was losing hope and helped her find her way when she got lost.

She was many things, including a deep feeler, overthinker and passionate lover ...

And one day, she knew she would also be in love – whether it was with herself or the person of her dreams.

She never stopped believing.

That was and always would be what made her truly magical.

There Is Hope in the Air, and You Are Loved

I know you've had a tough time lately, Darling, but you're going to be okay.
You've felt like the walls were closing in and nothing was going right, but with the change of seasons, comes a chance to change your story.
No matter how hard it is or what's holding you back, let it go and turn the page.
Don't be afraid of what the future may hold because there is beauty in the possibilities.
A new season, a new chapter, a new you.
The chance to rewrite your story lies in your hands.
Let go of the pain that's weighing you down.
Stop looking back: the past has nothing new to say.
This is your time ...
Time to change.
Time to grow.
Time to evolve.
You are loved more than you know, though I know it's easy to forget sometimes ...
When the weight of the world falls on your shoulders, you close your eyes and hope you

can keep going ... I know that feeling because I've been there, too.

Don't let the struggles define you and don't let your pain confine you –

Let the lessons you've learned refine you.

I know it's never easy walking away from people, places and things – even if you were never meant to hold onto them – but it's time to outgrow what's been holding you back.

You're meant for more, you're capable of more and you want more ...

So, make yourself a promise every day that you're going to keep your head high, your eyes bright and your heart open.

Take time for yourself and do the things that make you happy when you need it.

You can't pour from an empty cup.

So, as we celebrate the beauty of seasons changing, embrace the winds of opportunity that are beginning to blow.

I know it's scary taking steps in new directions, but you deserve more.

Pick up the pen.

Trust the magic of new beginnings ...

And let this be your season of beautiful blossoming.

You got this.

I'm Perfectly Flawed, and I Like It

I realize that I can be an absolute mess at times, it's just part of who I am.

I wish I could tell you that I was a simple person, but I'm anything but.

I'm a complex personality with a unique blend of qualities that may make your head spin sometimes.

At first glance, people think I'm a strong person, but those who really understand and love me know I'm a deep-feeling soul with a loving heart ... and I'm weak when it comes to the people I care about.

I know I'm not easy to understand, and I appreciate my people who get that I'm worth the effort.

I used to think I was an introvert, but the more I learned about myself the more I realized that I'm a little bit extrovert too ... it all just depends on my mood and who I'm with.

There are days when I feel like pulling my hair out and crying minutes before something hilarious makes me double over with side-splitting laughter.

That's the beautiful disaster that is me – you never know which version you'll get, and you

may even get both at the same time, so buckle up, Buttercup ... I'm always a heck of a ride.
Some may say I'm challenging, but I just call it interesting.
Anyone can be ordinary, average and routine ... I keep things a bit on the spicy side, though I don't do it that way on purpose.
You'll never really know what's going through my mind; I've learned to disguise my emotions masterfully – I'll often tell you that I don't care when the truth is I care too much.
I have the simple needs most people have – to love and be loved, to be understood and appreciated ...
I just happen to pursue those desires in extraordinary ways ...
With sass, pizzazz, and a lot of sarcasm sometimes too.
I call that my bold, fun flavor – tasty to those who love me and disconcerting to the rest ...
But I realized a long time ago that I would never be able to please everyone.
So, I stopped trying.
Better to make myself happy, fill my soul with joy and love my life and my people with all my heart.

If I can't put my whole heart and soul into something or someone, I'll do what's best for me and step away.

I know I'm awesome in all my flaws, and I embrace each of my dents, imperfections and scars fully.

They've made me who I am, and I'll never regret anything I've done or anywhere I've been.

I'm a big bundle of emotions, happiness and personality, and you'll never forget me once we've met.

Maybe you'll love me, maybe not ...

But I'll keep on dancing to my own beat, living in my own light and loving myself the best way I know how.

I like who I am, and I guess it's up to you to decide if you do too ...

I'll keep on doing what I do best regardless. Shining brightly.

A Weak Man Will Never Know What to Do with a Strong Woman

She's a strong woman with an intense personality, and she makes no apologies for who and what she is.

Men gush about how amazing she is, how they admire her strength and how they plan to pursue her with relentless intent ...

But the thing is, most of them just like the idea of her – the real and authentic woman she is will always be too much for most.

They don't truly understand her or what it takes to love a person like her.

Her needs and desires are simple enough – love, respect and loyalty. Ideals that are much more than words: they are tenets.

She's not one to be taken lightly or dismissed easily, for she goes after what she wants and doesn't know defeat.

So, while weaker men may dream, it takes a strong man to run with this lioness.

She's not content with lackluster character or ordinary passion.

She needs more. She craves the one who can ignite her heart and connect with her soul ...

And with the walls she has built around her inner depths, that's no easy task.

Many have tried and all have failed because she's not going to settle, wait or be just an option.

She demands the best of those who stay in her life, just as she gives ...

All of her heart, every bit of her soul and loyalty without end.

The ones who seek temporary satisfaction and superficial desire won't ever get a chance ... she knows the look and feel of a coyote in wolf's clothing.

She carries herself with dignity, class and courage and expects the same from any who would attempt to love her.

Some may push her away, saying she's overbearing, too demanding or too much ...

And she's fine with that. She would rather walk alone than pretend with the wrong one.

She'll never be happy with just anyone because she doesn't actually need anyone.

She loves herself completely and values her own time and independence ...

So, if someone wants to step up and vie for her affection, they'd better be prepared to be patient, true and genuine. Her world isn't one that tolerates insincerity.

She's been down that road too many times before, and she's never going back. That bridge has been burned.

She's always trusted that if love is meant for her, it will show up when the time is right ... and not a minute before.

So, as far as she's concerned, any man with false intentions can save his time, energy and shallow requests ...

She isn't stopping for just a distraction who would never be capable of earning her heart. Maybe she's tough – she is definitely strong – and she'll always be one of a kind ...

So, until someone comes along to run with her and win her heart, she'll just keep living her best life.

Always strong,

Always beautiful,

And always free.

Afraid of the Realness

I'm scared, just like you are.
I've never experienced anything like our love
before, not ever, not in any way.
Our connection is so powerful that I can't
explain how I feel, only that it's something I've
become sure of – like the sun rising or being
able to breathe.
I know you've never found someone you
couldn't live without before,
And that terrifies you.
You don't like the trust you're surrendering or
the vulnerability this creates between us.
I'm right there with you.
I never expected to find you. I never believed
that feelings of this magnitude even existed.
You've been hurt before, and I know your heart
can be fragile.
I also know that building the right foundation
will take time, patience and love ...
And I'm prepared to do whatever it takes to
protect your heart and show you that I'm for
real.
It's crazy really, how our lives collided into love.

We were two people content and living our best lives solo ... until this love story knocked on our doors and changed everything.

I didn't expect it, I still don't know what to make of it sometimes, but I'm embracing you, our love and our future with open arms.

So, we don't need to rush. Let's just walk for a while and get to know each other ...

Let's learn the language of our hearts, explore the connection of our souls, and truly dive deeper into this amazing gift that we've been blessed with.

I can't promise I'll always be perfect or that life will be easy, but if we work together, hold hands through the hard times and never stop loving each other openly and honestly, there's nothing we can't do ... together.

I've waited my whole life for you, so let's just build our trust, our lives and our future, one day at a time.

This is really happening, so let's pinch ourselves every so often and remind each other how much we love each other, every day in every way.

Scared, happy, excited, worried, blissful ...
All the things we both feel are normal and natural.

Let's just make sure that we do whatever we can ...
To communicate, to work together and to fall in love with each other all over again,
Every day.
My heart and soul will always be entwined and in love with yours ...
Forever starts today.

If I Let You In, Please Don't Break Anything

You say that you want the chance to know me,
to step beyond the walls I've built to protect my
heart, but that's a big step for me.
I've had my heart broken more times than I can
count, and I promised myself long ago that I
would always be careful who I let in.
So, if I choose to let you in, please don't break
anything ... like my heart.
Don't betray my trust.
Don't disrespect me.
Don't take me for granted.
Maybe those things sound insignificant to you,
but they're everything to me, because I've
been in a relationship where I didn't have those
things and it hurt ... a lot.
I deserve better.
I know my worth, and I'm not settling for
anyone who can't treat me the way I want.
My walls are high for a reason.
If you choose to truly connect with me, know
that my love, my trust and my heart must be
earned ... and I don't give those things lightly.
Know that I'm a complex person with a
sometimes-challenging demeanor, but it's just

because I've put myself back together again
after falling apart, and I'm stronger for it ...
Never assume you know who I am or what I'm
about until you truly make the effort to get to
know me.

I don't give just anyone access to my soul, so
tread carefully and be gentle, for my heart and
depths can be fragile ...

I'm willing to give you the chance to
understand me, if you choose, but it's not
lightly that I do so, and it has conditions.

Be honest, be true and always be transparent.
I don't play games, and I don't waste time
trying to guess intentions.

So, this is your chance to step up and venture
past my walls to finally unravel the mysteries
behind my eyes ... or to walk away if your
intentions aren't honorable.

This is who I am and what I want, so if you
choose to take my hand and walk with me, do
so with care.

If I'm letting you in, be gentle with my heart.
I'm trusting you with so much ...

Most of all, I'm trusting you to not break
anything.

I know I'm worth that and much more.
The question is ...

Do you?

I'm Tired of Fighting. My Silence Means I'm Moving On

I wish we weren't where we are, but we've tried everything.

Working through things, compromising, changing ...

We've fought so much that I don't even know what we were fighting about.

I'm weary – so far beyond exhausted – and I can't do this anymore.

So, I know you expected a fight when you called and started in on me, but I just can't – I have nothing left.

I'm done.

I don't have any fight left.

So, the best I can give you is my silence.

There's no more working through things, hashing them out or trying to figure it out.

We've done our best, and sometimes you just have to realize that it's not meant to be ...

And that's where I am.

I will always care about you, and you'll always have a special place in my heart, but that's where you belong: my heart, not my life.

I'm walking away knowing we've done all that we could, and it wasn't going to work out, no matter how much we tried ...

Sometimes, love alone just isn't enough.

We were like oil and water, regardless of how hard we loved.

So, my silence isn't about you or us anymore, it's about me ...

Trying to move on with dignity and grace, trying to heal from what's happened, trying to take the time to stop and make the changes I need to start finding my happiness again.

I realize you may never understand, and you'll chase me for a while, but sooner or later, you'll get it and maybe even agree it was for the best.

There are no right or wrong answers, just my heart trying to do the best thing for me.

It's hard,

It hurts,

But it's the right choice for both of us.

So, when I don't answer you or you don't hear from me anymore, know that this is the end of the road.

I'm telling you now ... and I hope for once you actually listen to me ... it's over.

It's one of the hardest things to do – letting go of someone you care about – but it's what needs to happen for us to both be happy again. Maybe you'll understand, maybe you won't. Either way, one day, I'll be fine ...
I always am.
My silence says everything my words never could ...
And now, it's saying goodbye.

I made a promise to myself that I would never
give up on my dreams.

There were a lot of times that I lost my way,
couldn't see the light and didn't know where to
go next.

I thought the magic of finding your dreams was
in reaching your destination, but that's not true
at all.

Every misstep, bad decision and poor choice
led me down the road I needed to take to build
a stronger character, forge a brave spirit and
learn what I was capable of.

I often wondered why I struggled so much and
why so many things went wrong, but that's
what I needed to experience to become the
person I am today.

I went through the fire to understand how to
rise again.

I failed and stumbled so I could learn how to
pick myself back up and keep going.

I chose the wrong people to love so I could
figure out how to be cautious in my choices.

I thought I had lost my magic and my way so many times that I didn't think I'd ever get where I was trying to go.

But that's the funny thing about life ...

It gives you what you need, when you need it ... but it doesn't always give you what you want.

But that's ok.

My goals and dreams don't have expiration dates, and there's no hurry to make things happen.

I've learned that people enter your life for a reason, a season or a lesson, and I've made the most of that knowledge.

I've found my tribe, my people, and I know that I'm never alone.

I've made it this far without always knowing where I was going because I never lost sight of who I wanted to become.

I valued the things that matter most to me: passion, character, authenticity and love.

Maybe they call me a dreamer, but I'm not the only one.

I've got light in my eyes and fire in my heart, so there's nothing I can't do if I put my mind to it.

I've been knocked down, failed and fallen, but I've never stopped believing in myself or my dreams.

Life isn't always grand or full of big moments, but I've learned to treasure the little things along the way: a beautiful friendship, a kind compliment, a warm drink on a chilly morning ... There's beauty all around, and I've finally stopped rushing and started taking it all in. There's no reason to hurry through life and miss all the little things that bring joy.

I know that I can realize my dreams while loving myself and my life ... just the way I want. Each and every day, I'll keep enjoying the journey, living my best life and loving myself and my people.

In the end, it's not about the number of breaths we take, but the moments that take our breath away ...

Starting with today.

The Heart Never Forgets

I came across a picture of you the other day,
and it made my heart skip a beat.
It'd been some time since I thought of you and
what we had, and I felt a strange mixture of
sadness and happiness.
It seems like just yesterday when you were the
most important thing in my life, the first person
I told everything to and my safe place every
day.
I don't really remember why we didn't work out,
and it's been so long, it doesn't really matter
anyway.
It was a love story that I thought would never
end – passionate nights and loving embraces
that made me feel like I was floating on air.
For a time, it was beautiful, it was love and it
was magical ...
I fought so hard to move on, burying the
memories and trying to forget ... though it took
me some time and healing to be okay with that.
I don't even know that I ever fully worked
through the pain of our split.
Until I saw your picture, I thought I had finally
gotten past everything, but I learned something
as the emotions washed over me.

We can forget, try to not think about or bury the memories of someone gone, of something painful ... but the heart never truly forgets.

So, as I looked at your picture, I wondered what you're doing. I even debated reaching out to you ... but I know that's not what's best.

Looking back will never help me build a better future for myself, so I'm just going to look ahead.

Seeing you created a myriad of emotions, but most of all, it reminded me of how hard I've worked to become a stronger, wiser and happier person ...

And nothing is worth sacrificing that, especially not the past.

I'll never be able to grab onto new hope and possibilities if I'm holding onto the pain of what's gone.

You'll always hold a special place in my heart, but not in my life.

So, I deleted your picture. I'm finally saying hello to my future and goodbye to my past.

It's a hard thing, moving on, but it's necessary for my growth and happiness.

Turning the page to a new chapter is always sad when people don't move on with you ...

But this time, I'm being true to myself.

That, for me, is all I could ask for.
I'm finally writing the story of my life the way I
always should have ...
Full of loving myself, seeking my own
happiness, and pursuing my dreams.

When You Can't Find the Light, I Will Hold Your Hand in the Dark

I know you've had a hard time lately, but I just want you to know that you are not alone.

Maybe you've lost your way, can't find the light or don't know where to turn ... and I get that.

I've been where you are more times than I can count, and it's hard to keep hoping and believing when you don't see the point.

It's easy to give up when you're mired in the dark and everything seems hopeless ...

But I'll tell you that it's darkest before the dawn – keep going.

And if you're weary, just need a rest or can't find the courage to start today, that's okay, too. I'll sit with you in the dark, hand in hand, until you're ready to begin again.

I know it's hard to find your way when you feel utterly lost, but take a deep breath and think about all those hopes and dreams you once had ...

They're still there, waiting for you.

I can't tell you it will get easy, or that the path ahead will be painless, but I can tell you that you can do it ... and that it's worth it.

But there's no rush and no reason to worry.

Let's sit for a while, me and you, and let's just talk.

About everything, about nothing.

About our hopes, dreams and everything in between.

After all, the beauty of life isn't the destination, but the joy of the journey itself.

So, let's take our time, enjoy the ride and just be ...

Be happy.

Be content.

Be still.

There's nothing wrong with resting for a while sometimes.

So, while we're pausing and catching our breath, let's just walk and talk for a while.

When you're ready, and the time is right, we can find our way, together ...

Just remember ...

You're never alone, and you matter.

You're enough ... so much more than enough.

You can do anything if you just start to believe ... I believe in you, now it's your turn ...

Will you join me?

The world and your dreams await.

The Price of Becoming Who You Are

Most people who meet her see a strong
person, capable of overcoming anything ...
They'll never realize the price she had to pay to
become the person that she is.
She started off much differently – bright eyed
and hopeful, she charged into the world with
her heart on her sleeve and light in her eyes ...
But life tried to take all that away from her, it
did everything it could to bring her to her
knees.
What the world didn't know was that behind the
thoughtful eyes and dreamer spirit was a
fighter – a brave soul who wouldn't accept
defeat and refused to let hardship tear her
apart.
While she still made bad choices and suffered
crushing heartbreak, she never pitied herself
nor wallowed in her failures.
She was better than that, for she knew the
challenges that lie in front of her and refused to
let life bring her down.
Maybe she wasn't ready for the fire that
scorched her soul, perhaps she didn't know
how hard her journey would become – loss and

pain can destroy some – but she never let her mistakes define her path.

She had promised herself from the very beginning never to lose sight of the things and people that mattered to her.

She managed to balance her outward toughness with a sensitive and loving heart in a world that doesn't easily let you be both.

That doesn't mean she didn't struggle with hard days or get down on herself, for there were days that she had to dig deep and claw her way through to the end ... but she always kept going.

Maybe she got frustrated a time or two, perhaps she cried a little when she felt overwhelmed sometimes, but you'd never be able to tell ...

For her beautifully placid eyes were the symbol of who she was and the hardy spirit that pushed her to keep getting up and looking up.

So, when the fires of life raged around her, she didn't just keep walking through the flames ... she became the fire.

When everyone else quit, she found a way to keep going and rising above – for she refused to quit or accept failure.

She was an unusual blend of a beautiful soul with both claws to dig herself out of the harshest battles and wings to fly high and chase her dreams.
She wasn't just a woman; she was a fighter with an unrelenting vision to become everything she ever wanted to be ...
And so that's the path she chose, rain or shine.
She kept showing up, stepping up and rising again.
One moment, one day and one dream at a time ...
She kept believing and evolving.
Beautiful, strong and free.

The Magnitude of My Light Is Measured by My Darkness

When you look at me and see my glowing smile and happy laugh, you think it's been easy for me ...
You couldn't be more wrong.
I've given everything I have to get to this place where all you see on my face is happy rays of sunshine.
There will always be storms brewing behind my soulful eyes, but not everyone cares enough to look closely ... and I'm good with that.
No, this hasn't been an easy road for me, and it still isn't ... but I've learned how to fall down with grace, rise again with courage and push forward with determination.
Oh, Darling, the darkness knows me all too well – it's got a room with my name on it, because I've visited there more than most ever will.
But I had to learn to embrace my darkness to appreciate the light, and I'd never change that about myself. In fact, I'd say that's one of the best things about me: I understand the balance of everything.

Until you've endured the pain, you'll never fully grasp the joy of happiness ... until you've dwelled in the dark, you can't truly appreciate the light ...

I'll always be a balance of both, and it makes me stronger and wiser.

I've known more pain and struggle than most will never visit, and I've overcome obstacles that many could never fathom.

Does that make me a survivor?

No. I'm more than a word, a label or a definition.

I'm the spark that burst into a wildfire, unwilling to settle for less and determined to become more.

I've battled my demons and silenced the voices of self-doubt ... though they often try to visit me in the serenity of night.

I'm an imperfect concoction of darkness and light, peace and struggle, pain and pleasure ... and I celebrate every flaw, bruise and dark moment for the lessons they have to teach me.

So, when you see my smile and wonder what I'm really like behind my eyes, deep down in my soul ... tread lightly.

I'm never going to be a little rainbow of happiness, but I'll always be real in ways you've never known.

I'm a beautiful mess who makes the best out of everything life throws at me ... and I wouldn't have it any other way.

Before you seek to unravel my mysteries, know that I'm an amazing soul with a heart of gold.

But unless you're willing to dance with my darkness a time or two, I might just be a little too much for you.

Either way, I love who I am and embrace who I'm becoming, each success, failure and beautiful moment in between.

I'm real, authentic and genuine ... every step of the way.

The question is ...

Are you really ready for my deepest truths?

But Will They Be Brave Enough to Fall for You?

She knew when they met that he was almost everything she had ever wanted ...

Only, it was the "almost" that turned the happy thoughts into sad moments.

A whirlwind romance, all the right words and magical nights swept her off her feet, and while she had promised herself to take it slow, she couldn't help but fall headfirst into love with him ... Yet, even as she spilled her heart to him, she realized that he wasn't strong enough to take the plunge.

She couldn't tell if it was fear, uncertainty or just apathy, but he couldn't return her love. Confused, she poured back over their time together, trying to see what she had done wrong or if she had misread the situation. Nothing.

Love was a complex emotion, she knew, and she was patient ... after all, he'd shown her that he cared for her.

Why the hesitation? Why the uncertainty? She studied his face, searching for an answer that would never come ...

He wouldn't commit and couldn't even tell her why.

Her heart sank as she realized that she had fallen for someone who wasn't brave enough to fall for her ...

She deserved a love that was courageous enough to risk it all to be with her ...

And that just wasn't him.

It probably would never be him.

Maybe he was scared of commitment, perhaps he didn't know what he wanted ...

She didn't know for sure.

But what she did know was that she wasn't the type of person to wait on someone to "figure it out."

She made the choice that was the hardest she'd ever known and walked away, battling her heart every step of the way.

Better to leave now with her dignity and self-respect than to sacrifice her values to chase someone unsure of his feelings.

She deserved better than that, so she was taking back her destiny and putting her happiness back into her own hands.

Sure, she'd have some sleepless nights and cry her fair share of tears, but this was the only choice ...

He knew where she was, and she wasn't waiting around anymore on someone that may never come around.

What's meant to be will always find a way, and she was making her own way now.

It would be hard, it would be sad for a moment, but she'd be fine ...

She always was.

And this time, she'd not make the same mistake twice.

She'd hold out for the one whose love matched her own ...

Or she'd keep living her best life and loving herself ...

Because that was one love she could always be sure of.

Love lost is a hard lesson, but it was one she learned well.

New days, new chapters and always, a new chance to find herself ...

Love will do what it wants anyway.

Might as well tackle everything else on her own terms.

A Self Renovation

That me that you used to know?
Yeah, that person is gone now.
I had a lot of stuff weighing me down, and I
couldn't keep going the way that I was ...
So, I did the hardest thing I've ever done and
renovated myself – improved, evolved and
grew the parts that needed to catch up to the
me that I want to be.
Yes, that's right. You probably won't recognize
this version of me anymore, because it's way
better than that disaster that I used to be ...
Going from mistake to mistake and loving all
the wrong people ... I'm amazed I'm still in one
piece.
But here I am, renovated, elevated and
dedicated to improving myself.
No, I'm not going to let you or anyone else
treat me the way that you used to – I'm better
than that, and I deserve more.
I'm raising the bar, my standards and my head
as I start changing the game in my favor.
I'm tired of losing at life, falling flat on my face
and feeling hopeless all the time.

So, excuse me if I don't have time for people who used to disrespect me, mistreat me or brush me aside.

If you want to step to my new level, then you'll need a taller ladder this time.

I'm still the same wonderful soul behind my fiery eyes, but now, I'm expecting more, giving more and never giving up.

Maybe you can handle that, maybe you can't.

Either way, I'm going to keep evolving to get better every day ...

So, I know you think you know me, but I can promise you that I'm not the person you knew.

I'm stronger.

I'm wiser.

And I'm so much better than I ever was before.

Change is inevitable, but evolution is optional ... So, I chose to evolve.

What are you choosing?

You've been stuck in the same place for too long, Darling ...

You've wanted to find your wings and soar, but the world has kept you down.

The doubts, the fears and the worries can be overwhelming, I know ...

Turn the page and start a new chapter.

This is a story that you control, and you can change.

No, it won't be easy, fast or painless, though it will be worth it.

But first, you must find a way to believe ...

In yourself, in the process, in your journey – whatever it takes to help you take one step, then another.

Let go of the people who have been holding you back – you know, the ones who would have you always stay the same for their benefit.

They don't want you to grow, evolve and get better ... they want you to remain unchanged just like they are ...

After all, misery loves company.

You've heard the quiet voice in the back of your mind whispering, haven't you?

It's telling you that you can be more, that you're meant to do more ...

But you've been afraid to listen, I know.

Change is hard, especially when you don't know where you're going or how.

The best part is, though, you don't have to.

You just have to start improving the parts of yourself that have been aching to break free.

If evolution were easy, everyone would do it.

Listen to your heart and follow your passion – it knows the way.

Enrich your mind, enflame your spirit and dig deep for that bravery to step out of the comfort zone you've been content to dwell in for far too long.

Read a book. Take a course. Make a trip to somewhere new. Do the things that fill your soul and awaken your sleeping spirit.

You've wanted this for so long, waiting for a sign to break free of the patterns that have held you captive ...

This is it.

Take the chance.

Seize the day.

Open your mind and embrace the possibilities of new people, places and adventures.

Let go of the pain and burdens you've been carrying for so long.
Most of all, spread your wings ...
You have better places to fly.
I believe in you.
Fly high, Darling ... the future's waiting.
And it all begins with you.

Every Person Is a Lesson, and That Is What Matters

It took me a long time to understand that not everyone that I had feelings for or connected with would always stay in my life.

When you happen upon special feelings, whether they are friends or partners, you hold on to those emotions because they grab a special place in your heart ...

But then, as I watched friends disappear and love walk away, I realized that not everyone is in your next chapters – sometimes, they happened into my life to teach me something.

It was up to me if I was strong and wise enough to take in the teachings a person was there to impart.

Looking past the pain of my loss was the hardest thing I could do, but as I started to understand that what is meant to be will always find a way, it just clicked.

People would come into my life for a season, a reason or a lesson ... the rest that stayed?

Well, those were my people – the ones I love without condition, the loyal loves that are part of my circle.

It's not easy saying goodbye to people who choose another path, but I had to learn that it is part of the journey.

I'll always remember the ones who left, what they meant and what I learned from them ... whether it was never to settle for less than I deserve, or even to never assume someone feels the same way I do.

Everything and everyone has meaning. It's up to me to find it.

I've stopped worrying about the things I can't control, what other people do and say, and what tomorrow holds.

I have enough on my plate without fretting unnecessarily ... so I'm not doing that anymore.

I'm sure I'll still have nights where sleep is fleeting, and there will be days when I'm just trying to keep moving forward ...

But that's part of my path, my growth.

Change isn't easy and people leaving is hard, but I'm starting to breathe easier and accept better the things that I can't control.

One day at a time, small victories and joy in the moments – that's what I'm focusing on.

I'll find where I'm meant to be, I'll keep evolving from the lessons learned and people I've loved.

At least now, in my life, I'm living it my way.

The Love You Give

I know you've had your heart broken,
I realize that the ones that promised
That they'd never leave or forsake you,
Walked away and broke your heart.

It's been a hard path for you,
Wanting to believe in love,
Yet too hurt and broken to give in,
Building the highest walls to protect your heart.

I'm here now, standing before you,
Because I see the pain shrouded behind
The beautiful eyes that hide your depths
And I'm willing to take the time ...

To earn your trust, respect and love ...
By protecting your heart,
Loving you unconditionally
And standing beside you, always.

I believe in meant to be,
That our paths were always going to cross,
Our love was inevitable, and we were destined,
But now, the rest of the journey is up to us.

Take my hand, and let's just take our time:
To walk, talk and learn about each other.
Our hopes, our dreams and everything in
between.
Taking down the walls, piece by piece.

As I look into your beautiful eyes,
I know why I'm here as love fills my heart.
Know that every day, for the rest of our lives,
It will forever be us – me and you ...
Loving, living and laughing for always.

A Wildflower in a Word Full of Roses

In a world full of people trying to be the same
kind of beautiful, she chose to be herself.
Maybe it wasn't what everyone else aspired to
emulate or become, but that didn't matter to
her.
While they were out chasing attention, affection
and popularity, she sought much simpler
things:
Happiness, peace, love ... all the ideals that the
world told her weren't real or important.
She dared to believe differently.
Not to be contradictory, but because that's
what mattered to her.
Listening to her heart, marching to her own
beat and following her passion were part of
who she was ...
Perhaps she was utterly too real in a world that
fawned over fakeness, but she was quite
content to be her own version of authentic.
Others would scoff as she embodied old
fashioned values and believed in love, but
she'd just smile and keep on her merry way.
She knew that they didn't really see her for
who she was, and she was good with that ...

she wasn't interested in being trendy, popular or cool.

Her people – the ones who truly understood her – loved every bit of her unapologetically real personality and sometimes brash uniqueness.

The rest didn't matter to her, for most never even saw past the facade she wanted them to see.

She was beautiful, not like you and me, but in ways that were pure, wholesome and undeniable.

She was unafraid to love despite the risk, and she knew the feeling of heartache just as well ... but that didn't change how much she loved love.

Road trips to nowhere, long midnight conversations and dancing in the kitchen were part of her wild spirit that the world couldn't tame ...

No matter how hard they tried.

She was determined to keep dancing, keep loving and keep flying high so long as she had breath to give ...

In a world full of roses and thorns,
She would always be a beautiful and uninhibited wildflower.

And I Choose You

From worlds apart and miles away,
We found each other against all odds.
Love was never in our sights,
But it was intent on uniting you and me.

We were content in our lives,
Chasing our dreams the best we could ...
Only we never knew that we were missing
That connection we found in us.

From the first word, the first laugh,
The very first moment we knew,
Everything changed in us and our lives.
We suddenly needed something never known:
Each other.

I can't say I've ever felt a power like this,
A hunger for your love like I know now,
Only that I'm incomplete without you,
Needing you every day in every way.

In that singular moment when I found you,
It all changed when you became my
everything.
Nothing would ever be the same,

Nor would I want it to be.

You're my happy place at day's end,
The kiss that welcomes me home,
A burning to be in your arms,
That eclipses the need for all else.

So, as we embrace and the world melts away,
Know that it is these moments I treasure,
Our love suspended in beautiful bliss ...
Soulmates, best friends, twin flames, partners
...
Forever and always, 'til time is no more.

She Was a Warm Embrace, His Reminder of Beauty in the World

No matter how hard life could be, she was always waiting for him, arms open –
The warm embrace at the end of a sometimes-cold day, reminding him that his safe place was forever in his arms.
Though they parted every morning to pursue their various endeavors, they never lost their beautiful connection, for they always carried their love with them, no matter how far they traveled.
A simple text, quick call or little nudges of love between them always kept their fire burning when the world tried to quench the spark.
There were always moments when life brought them to their knees, but together, hand in hand, they always found their way and their strength to push forward ...
Never losing their special bond, for that was the essence of their souls.
They both knew that she was his fire, and he was her rock, and their hearts beat as one, even as the world could come crashing down around them.

In a life that did everything to tear them apart and destroy their love, they always found each other and nurtured the beauty of their connection, each and every day.

Maybe it wasn't perfect or full of grandiose moments, but it was real, it was true, and more than anything,

It was the two of them, loving each other in their own special way.

Some of our love stories may be a little dented and scratched, but they're every bit as beautiful as the fairytales.

Because they're our own special love, told in a beautiful way that only we will know and appreciate.

And that's the most wonderful part of all.

Stuck

It's those times at night when I'm lying in bed lost in thought that are the hardest.
My mind has races thinking about what has been, what will be and even what could be ... and it's almost overwhelming at times.
I wish I could stop turning over the endless possibilities and thinking about the painful past, but that's just how my mind works.
I've been hurt so many times it almost feels normal now, and I've been broken apart so often, I just want to forget how broken I am.
I try to embrace my flaws, mistakes and pain to become better, but it's just so hard to overcome the feelings that bring me down.
All the emotions, thoughts and pain blend together, and so often I'm stuck between wanting to come apart completely and trying to forget the people and hurt that led me to this place.
I fight to focus on evolving from the lessons of my past, but sometimes, I get stuck and can't move forward ... I'm just mired in the darkness.
In the silence of the night the quiet can be deafening, and that's when it's the hardest ...

Alone with my thoughts with nothing but sleep – which can be so fleeting – to keep me from the darkness.

It's hard to forget, to let go and to move on ... but I'm trying.

I know that I have to make peace with my pain and confront my demons in order to make my angels sing – and I know that won't be easy or fast – but I'm determined to rise out of the angst and find my way back to the light.

So, yeah, maybe I'm broken, but I'm not too shattered to start again and put my pieces back together in a better way.

I'm beautiful in the way the broken fragments of my heart and soul come together now, and I'll keep rising until I'm able to feel the joy again.

Broken doesn't mean lost, it means starting again ... and that's just what I'm doing.

It may not be tomorrow, next week or next month, but I'll get there ...

One way or another.

I'm grabbing my happiness and I'm not letting go.

Broken, beautiful and just doing my best every day ... that's me.

No matter how I get knocked down or stuck I get ...
I got this.

Somewhere along the way, I lost myself and my magic that had once meant so much to me. I really couldn't tell you how or when, only that the little sparkle in my eye that used to inspire me just started to disappear.

Maybe it was life and all its challenges, maybe it was the broken hearts I endured chasing love ...

I really couldn't tell you.

But one day, I realized I wasn't the person I had set out to be, and I wasn't okay with that anymore.

I had been simply existing and not thriving for so long, I had lost my way.

It's hard to recover that spark that makes your passions burn brightly when it's gone ...

But I knew that I had to dig deep, revitalize my spirit and find the girl I used to be who had been missing for far too long.

The one that loved music as it filled her soul, inspiring her to dance and lose herself to the rhythm ... at peace as she immersed herself in song.

I stopped rushing and started truly paying attention to the beauty all around me in my life

... it had been there all along, I just got too busy living life for all the wrong reasons.

The more I started to rekindle the things that moved my soul and stoked my heart, the more that girl came out and reminded me who I once was so long ago ...

The girl who dreamed endlessly, loved intensely and saw the beauty and magic in everything and everyone around her.

The person who would roll her windows down and turn her music up, letting the breeze billow through her hair as she let go of the world and reveled in the moment.

Little by little, day by day, that girl started to stop by more often and stay a little longer each time ...

In fact, I think she's found that magic that she misplaced long ago.

Who knows?

Maybe one day soon, she'll even remember her wings and find the courage to fly again as she once did ...

And she can't wait to soar.

I think this time, that girl might just stick around for a while.

Tell That Woman in the Mirror That She Deserves the Best Kind of Life

I found myself staring into the mirror on the verge of tears, almost unable to recognize the woman staring back at me.

The fine wrinkles around my eyes told the story of a life marked with struggle and strife ... one that I had fought in search of my happiness.

And I had never quit, never stopped believing. Joy seemed fleeting sometimes, and I had spent too many sleepless nights overthinking and worrying about things I couldn't control,

But as I looked closer at my face, I could make out the barely discernible lines from laughter and love once shared, though that now seemed so far away.

That was the woman I had to find again, the spirit I needed to rekindle once more.

I knew that I needed and deserved more, that I was meant for more – I had just lost my way trudging through the failures and heartache of love lost and friends gone.

Truth was, I had spent so long staring backwards at what was gone that I had forgotten how to look ahead at the possibilities.

I had lost sight of what I wanted to become and what I wanted from life because my hands were still full of yesterday's baggage.

I didn't want to look in the mirror anymore and see someone unrecognizable – I wanted to look at myself and feel proud of the woman I had worked to become.

So, I'm making up my mind to move past the scars that tell my story because I'm not letting them define me any longer.

I'm choosing to let go of the weight of the world that I can't control and focus on the things in my life that I can control.

I know it's going to be the battle of my life, but I'm worth it ... and I can do it.

My life, my happiness and my peace are worth any price that I have to pay.

If I can't find it within myself to start healing and begin to love me again, how can I expect anyone else to?

I'm done feeling sorry for myself, accepting failure and wallowing in the darkness.

Forget the wings, I've got claws, and I'm digging myself out of this anguish and climbing back to myself ...

Back to a happier me.

I'm prepared to walk through the fire and stand strong through the rain, because the storms of this life have already tried to destroy me ...

And they failed.

I'm still standing.

I'm still smiling.

I'm getting stronger every day.

I'm turning the page and starting a new chapter.

I can't change the beginning, but I can rewrite where my story goes from here.

I'm worth it, I'm more than enough, and I'm rising from the ashes.

Phoenix reborn and forged in the flames, I'm turning my setbacks into a comeback.

No matter what, regardless of how long it takes or where the road leads me,

One thing will always be true:

I'm not a survivor, I'm a warrior.

And this time, I'm not staying down.

I'm setting my heart on fire and blazing a new path to a better me.

I'm not stopping 'till I reclaim my joy and stand proud seeing that woman in the mirror that I fought to become ...

This is my time ... I got this.

The Strength to Love a Broken Woman

She knows she's not the easiest person to love because she's become a bit cynical after not having had the best luck.

Not because she doesn't believe in love or in finding her soulmate, but because she's kissed a lot of frogs hoping they were the one ...

And they may have seemed like a prince for a time, but eventually they all transformed for the worse after she let them in.

She had the worst luck in love, she often lamented, as her choices were more aptly projects not partners.

Her high walls were the result of a broken past, broken hearts and broken roads ...

And she was left to put it all together by herself ...

Which she did, stronger each time.

She never asked for help as she clawed her way back to what most would call a normal life ...

She called it a rebirth.

She knew that many would never realize the battles she'd fought just to get where she was, and she was fine with that ... she fought for herself, not for attention.

She didn't want pity; she wanted respect for the person she'd worked hard to become.

But as much as she grew, she would never forget where she'd been, the pain she'd felt or the tough climb she'd made.

So, when he came into her life unexpectedly, he saw the woman in front of him for the wonderful soul that she was ... and instantly knew that she would be worth the effort to earn her love, her trust, her respect ... and ultimately, a future together.

It wouldn't be an easy undertaking, for her walls were high and her trust was wary.

She refused to allow just anyone to get close enough to burn her again, for she had promised herself that she would be certain of the next one ... no more imposters, players or fakes would ever be allowed to hurt her again. She'd done that dance too many times, and she had thrown away those dancing shoes long ago.

She was playing for keeps, and whether someone came along or not, she wasn't settling, sacrificing or watering herself down. She didn't need anyone to make her whole – she was quite content on her own – but she'd

welcome the right person into her heart ...
cautiously.

Most of them called her demanding or high
maintenance, but he saw her differently ...

He could catch glimpses of the beautiful soul
protected behind her placid eyes, and he knew
where he belonged – with her.

No matter how long it took or the sacrifices he
would need to make ...

She was worth any price, and that's what he
knew he had to do.

For it takes strength to love a broken woman ...

And even more strength to love a woman like
her –

One who had put herself back together again
all on her own.

And he looked forward to spending the rest of
his life loving her just the way she'd always
wanted ... one day, one love, and one moment
at a time.

Today is a day just like any other, except for one difference.

I'm making a choice.

I'm tired of standing still. I'm tired of complaining about my life and not doing anything about it.

I've been stuck in this place for so long – just surviving my days – that I don't know if I can even find my way out.

But I have to try.

I can't accept being unhappy and miserable anymore, so today, I've decided to start doing instead of just talking.

I'm stepping out of my comfort zone – the place where I just go through the motions –and I'm stepping up my game.

You know what?

I'm absolutely terrified.

I'm scared of change, of failing, of not knowing where I'm going or what I'm doing.

Most of all, I'm scared of losing my way and never finding my way back.

I know it's going to hurt, and I may not always know how I'll keep pushing forward ...

236

But I have to.

I want to be happy again.

I deserve to be happy.

I've let others dictate who I am and what should make me happy for far too long, so I'm starting now ...

I'm taking back my voice and setting boundaries.

I'm taking back my standards, and I'm setting the bar where I want it.

I'm taking back my life and charting a new path.

I'm done looking over my shoulder, carrying the burden of past pain and mistakes.

I'm done letting yesterday weigh me down.

I'm raising my standards, my head and my hopes to a new level, and I won't accept anything less than what I'm worth ...

Because I'm worth it all, I'm more than enough, and I got this.

I know I'm going to be scared with every step and unsure of where to go next ... but that's just a part of growth.

My voice may tremble as I make myself heard, but I'm starting to make my way.

The uncertainty, the doubt, the worries ... they have shackled me all my life, and I can't live that way anymore.

I won't live that way anymore.

Maybe I won't make big strides immediately, it may take me some time to figure out what I'm doing ... but that's okay.

Life is about the journey, not the destination.

I'm done looking at the road signs to where I've been, instead I'm looking ahead for where I'm going.

So, yes, today is a day like any other, but it's also a day like no other.

I chose today to change my life, my mindset and my future ...

Starting now.

With me.

I'm scared, but I got this.

Take my hand, let's rise up and start our journey to a better place ...

One where dreams come true and happiness is real.

Me and you, let's start now.

But first ... we must believe.

The Gentleman Who Will Open Your Heart

She yearned for more than ordinary, in fact, she craved it.

There was a time when love seemed so impossible, when her heart was too often broken and cast aside – but that's when she learned what kind of man that she wanted.

Not a man that you found every day, but one of the truly special kind –

The type that, if you were lucky, you happened upon by chance.

Sure, there were plenty of men out there, and many handsome ones at that, but she knew she needed more than the average man.

Good enough wasn't enough for her now.

Handsome was nice but fell short of her desires – she required much more than an attractive face.

She yearned to find that extraordinary man – the gentleman who strove to be more, to do more and who saw her for who she truly was … a gentleman whose quality of character and honorable heart would leave you awestruck.

He was the kind of man who saw beyond her exterior into the depths of who she truly was.

She didn't need any man, just the contrary,
only a gentleman wolf of extraordinary caliber
would do.
She wanted a man with a strength to match her
own, passion to light her heart and the courage
to run wild with her.
She waited for the day one would show up with
more than simple wants and dreams.
Simplicity is well and good, she thought, but
not in her forever love.
She needed a complex man with singular
tastes: passion, love, character and respect.
Simple just wasn't who she was, and it would
never define her.
So, until a man showed up in her life that got
her and possessed the patience to delve
deeper into her truths, she'd not waste her time
with lesser men full of overblown egos and
superficial desires.
She wanted her mind romanced.
She needed her soul uncovered.
She longed for her heart to be stoked.
He would come in spectacular fashion, and, in
an instant, in a glance, she'd just know.
He'd taste her words with hungry anticipation,
waiting for each syllable with sumptuous
desire.

He would make love to her mind and claim her soul with a reckless pursuit of her truths.

He'd unfold her story, and his need for more would make him intensely passionate.

That, she knew, was the man she wanted, needed and awaited.

Anything less was just a boy dressed up in nice clothes.

And she'd take nothing less than a man – her man, her gentleman.

Until then, she'd wait for him ...

Her love, her soulmate, her gentleman wolf ... in her dreams.

When Your Heart Understands There Is No Turning Back

She lay in bed crying, caught in the middle of that hard battle between heart and mind.
He had made his choice and did so in the worst possible way.
He didn't come to her and talk to her about how he felt ... he sought the arms of another.
She had loved him for so long, and finding out that way shook her to her core.
She was a confused mess of anger and sadness ... she had no words for the way she felt at that moment.
She wanted to scream at him, unleash the overwhelming rage she felt for his deceitful choice ... but she knew that would do no good.
He had tried to apologize, told her all the things he thought she wanted to hear ... but she wasn't the type of woman who tolerated infidelity.
There was nothing he could say or do that would change her mind about what she knew she had to do ...
But her heart – the one part of her that wouldn't let her close the door fully – still loved him,

wanted to believe in him, and longed to give him another chance.

Deep down, she knew she had no choice but to let him go ...

But that didn't make letting go any easier. She caught herself looking at old pictures of them together, transporting her back to a happier time – when their love was young, and the future seemed limitless.

Wiping away a tear, fighting to pull herself together, she picked up her phone and typed out a message.

Finishing the text and pressing send, she was overwhelmed with a combination of relief and sadness ...

Actually, much more than that, but those were the emotions that struck her first.

Her heart pounded and she fought to catch her breath as she stared at the message she had just sent to him.

She was doing what she knew had to be done, but it didn't make it any easier.

With those few words, she had made her choice.

What she sent him was more than just a message for him, it was a statement to herself that she was closing this chapter of her life.

If she talked to him again, she feared she would give in – she wasn't strong enough, she still cared about him, and the wounds were too fresh ...

Her heart wasn't ready to let go.

So, she sent him a message that gave her the start to a new path ...

Which scared and excited her at the same time ... "I'm done ..."

Now, with a few simple words, she was free.

It would be a hard few weeks and months ahead, but with determination, courage and healing ...

She'd be happier, eventually.

Looking forward to better days made a slight smile creep over her face.

That, for now, would have to be enough.

Free to find her own way ...

Back to the light.

Back to herself and happiness.

I Would Wait for You Forever

I never meant to fall in love with you, but when
I saw you, I never stood a chance.
You smiled and stole my heart before I realized
I had fallen for you.
I never really stood a chance, but then, I didn't
really want to.
You blew in like a whirlwind and ripped my
defenses asunder, and I was yours – with a
beautiful smile and a sumptuous kiss.
Loving you wasn't even an option, because
when your soul called to mine across a
windswept plane, I fell completely head over
heels for you.
Your words careened across my skin with
precocious splendor,
And your lips upon mine seduced me with a
fiery passion that I have never known.
As the days have passed and our hearts have
begun to beat as one,
I realized more and more how very familiar
you've always been to me.
We were never strangers from the moment we
met,
We just hadn't found each other yet in this
lifetime.

I knew when I looked in your eyes that our love was timeless – without beginning or end.

Mate of my soul, you have been my twin flame since before the chapters of time ever turned the first page.

Head to heart to spirit to soul, we've loved each other across countless times and endless places.

Against impossible odds, we've always found our way back to each other's arms.

Our love has endured when all else failed,

Your touch has always electrified my senses and calmed my restless spirit.

More than just butterflies and sweet whispers,

You've been my reason for being and my light in the darkness.

I'll hold your hand in mine as we face the world and years together,

And I'll find you once more in the next life ...

Even if I have to wait a hundred years to love you again,

I'd count the minutes until you were there,

Knowing that my forever begins and ends ...

With you.

I'd gladly wait for a hundred years if it meant you would find me at the end.

Each and every time.

That's love.
That's true.
That's us.
We are and always will be forever in love.

When a Woman Is Silent

She sits there, quiet ... lost in her thoughts.
Her face shows no emotion, for her stoic
facade is the face she's perfected.
She has built the incredible strength to tuck
away even the fiercest emotions behind the
demeanor of a steel warrior.
Her strength, built from walking through the
fires of life, isn't obvious at first glance ...
No, it's made up of the quiet courage and
bravery that many would probably miss about
her.
But her people – the ones who love her –
appreciate that about her so very much.
That's not to say she doesn't burst into tears in
the shower or face down into a pillow
sometimes, but she recomposes herself just as
quickly, wiping away the tears and pulling
herself back together.
She's a beautiful creature in her quiet virtue,
able to maintain her composure when the
world is crashing down around her.
She feels the same emotions you and I do, yet
somehow, she's able to harness her self-
control and measure her responses very
calmly ...

She may overthink situations, she may be falling apart inside or on the verge of tears, but she decides when to open the floodgates of emotion to release her heart.

Not just anyone is privy to such things, for she values her time and chooses her companions carefully.

She's careful with her heart and her love, for she's been burned before and has vowed to be selective when letting her walls down.

Truth be told, there's nothing in this world as extraordinary as a strong woman ...

She fights battles few ever know and chooses which mountains to climb and which to simply walk around.

So, if she's without words, know that a myriad of emotions may be swirling inside her heart and mind.

You may not be able to fully understand who she is or how she manages a smile through hardship, but one thing is for certain:

You're witnessing one of the most beautiful people you'll ever meet as you look upon her ...

Appreciate her, cherish her, and most of all, love her for the extraordinary person she is ...

A strong and resilient woman.

Show Me Your Truth and then Let Me Love You

Darling, come experience this life with me in the wildest and most amazing ways we can find.

Leave behind all the worldly stuff and let's just be us for a while ... no, change that ... not just for a time, but for forever.

Kiss me in the rain and hold my hand as we dance through the puddles of life ...

Don't let me go, ever – no matter how hard the storms come.

Turn up the music we love and let's pretend like we're giving the concert of our lives ...

Let's sing at the top of our lungs and not care who is watching or listening ...

This is our life and our love; we don't need anyone's permission or approval to be our silliest selves and love each other in just the ways we want.

In truth, that's what I want from you, all the time in all the ways.

Show me who you really are – bare your soul to mine so that we will never lose that connection that makes our love so special.

Tell me the truth, even when I don't want to hear it ... because that's what you'll always get from me.

Sure, I'm human, and I'm going to make mistakes – we both will ...

But that doesn't change how we feel or the love we have ... it just makes our love stronger through the ups and downs.

So, take my hand and let's do all the things the world says we shouldn't.

Road trips to nowhere for no reason other than to just enjoy each other.

Laying in a field under a star-filled sky, holding hands and talking for hours.

Rainy days with the music turned up full blast so that we can dance throughout the house ... In the kitchen, living room or on the patio outside – let the moonlight serenade our love.

Because Darling, we are one of a kind and meant to be, and there's no force on earth that can keep our love from blossoming.

So, let's lose ourselves in the life, the love and the laughter that fills our souls.

I've waited my whole life to hold your hand in the rain ...

We might as well dance in it while we're here.

I'm a Unique Blend of Wonderful Authenticity

Please understand that I'm an imperfect person who makes mistakes, loves completely and listens to my heart.

I'm broken in beautiful ways, and I always try to do my best, even if I fail sometimes.

I'm a unique blend of personality, stubbornness and wonderful authenticity.

I don't mean to say awkward things or make inappropriate jokes, I just have a bad habit of speaking before I think sometimes ...

But I'm continually working to improve myself and grow in the ways that matter.

I'm always real, to the point and down to earth, even if I'm still a dreamer at heart.

I believe in true love, meant to be and soulmates, and I'll never stop trying to catch my dreams.

I get lost in the music so often I forget where I am as the songs permeate my soul ...

That's just part of who I am and the magic that fills my heart.

I've learned to embrace and appreciate my flaws after a long journey to self love ...

And I have found the path to growth, evolution and always wanting to become more.

I stopped following the trends and the crowds long ago, for I walk away from fake and I don't care about what's cool.

My version of cool is probably a lot different than everyone else's anyway:

Long conversations about everything and nothing, dancing to the music that moves us, doing the things that push us out of our comfort zone ... those are a few of the ideals I chase with relentless optimism.

So, maybe I am a hodgepodge of beautiful disasters stitched together by deep quotes and meaningful thoughts ...

But I'm always true to my word, and I do what I say.

No matter where life leads me, I'll always follow my heart, believe with passion and dream with reckless abandon.

I'm not perfect, I'm not flawless,

But I am one of a kind ...

Here's to hoping you're down for the magical ride that is life.

She knows all the reasons to be careful with her heart, but she still loves with reckless abandon.

She knows who she is … she's a woman who believes in love, though it drives her friends crazy that she loves more than she'll ever get back.

She takes the risks knowing the pain that often waits on the other side of love gone wrong.

Nothing will dissuade her from following her heart.

She's not foolish and she's far from naive – just the opposite, in fact.

She's strong and resilient in ways most will never know, and she refuses to live or love small, because she's holding out for her forever.

She's going to kiss however many frogs it takes, turn the page of her love story as many times as she needs to so that she'll find her meant to be.

The difference between her and so many others is that she doesn't need a man at all … though she craves fulfilling companionship, she longs to share the joys of life with her special someone.

If love never comes knocking, she'll be quite content to love herself, her friends and her life just the way it is ...

But that doesn't mean she won't give her all in pursuit of her true love.

She doesn't know anything other than passion, love and soulful depth – they're an integral part of who she is, and she'll never deny her truths or shy away from a chance to love someone.

She knows what she deserves, and she'll never settle ... but she's strong enough to handle the pain and risk that can come with romance.

Most would swear off trying, saying it isn't worth it, but she's not one of those people.

She's got a heart of gold and wears her feelings on her sleeve ...

Unafraid to plunge headfirst into the madness of love ...

Because she made herself a promise long ago that no matter how hard life tested her, what people said or the heartache she had to endure, she wouldn't give up on love.

So, she won't.

There will never come a day for her when she has to say "if only ..."

So, she may give more love than she'll ever get back, but she'll keep loving anyway.

She's strong, beautiful and believes in love ... And she wouldn't have it another way.

The Day Is Yours, Make Magic with It

Darling, you've been living day to day too long,
struggling to find the time and energy to stop
for a bit and breathe.
It's time to turn the page and start a new
chapter ...
You know, the one where you celebrate you.
Forget what's gotten you down and let's put
aside the troubles that challenge you ... if only
for a little while.
Take a deep breath, it's time you did the things
that fill your soul and energize your spirit.
Stop making excuses for why you can't take
the time for yourself ...
You can't pour from an empty cup.
Get dressed up and feel good about yourself,
just because you want to.
Have a dance party in your kitchen – just you,
the music and freedom.
Don't tell me you can't or that it's not possible.
It's your life ... choose to make a change.
Choose to celebrate yourself and your life.
Take a drive to nowhere with the windows
down and the music up ...
It doesn't even have to be a grand adventure.
The little things matter so much too.

Go for a walk, read that book you've been putting off ...

Pay attention to the beauty all around you and don't take anything for granted.

You've been stressed, worried and tired for too long ... It's time to make time for yourself.

You deserve it.

No, more than that ... you've earned it.

You don't owe anyone an explanation for wanting to enjoy your life.

Feel the warm afternoon breeze blow through your soul as you immerse yourself in the moments that rekindle your fire ...

Big, little and everything in between, take the chance to fall in love with being alive again.

Once today's gone, you'll never get it back, so make it count.

Really live – stop just existing.

Only you have the power to master the clock, slow time and harness the positive energy that is all around you, just waiting for you to breathe life into it.

Today is yours and yours alone – seize the moments and find your magic again.

You've got one chance at this life ...

Open your wings and find the courage to fly again.

It's your time to shine, Darling ...
So, shine brighter than you ever have before.
You deserve it.

He didn't immediately realize how amazing she was. She seemed like any other woman at first glance ...

Until he looked closer.

Her soulful eyes brimmed with a beautiful depth that he had never experienced ...

And one look was all it took to crash his defenses.

He knew from that first moment that she was the one, though he could never have known how broken she was ... or how strong.

From a life of hardship and broken promises, she had struggled to find her way.

And though it had been hard, she had remained resilient and determined ... carefully preserving and protecting her smile in the process.

Even when she was dying inside.

She had lost confidence in herself in so many ways, looking in the mirror and only seeing the scars of the struggles she had endured.

But amidst her pain, he could see the beautiful soul just wanting to come out; he just had to help her find her way.

He wanted, more than anything, for her to see herself through his eyes for the amazing woman she was.

She had lost her way, so he did what he knew he must ...

He took her hand, walked with her and just patiently loved her ... he helped fill her up with the beautiful emotions he felt inside.

Slowly and surely, she began to make her way back home, back to her true self that she had let the others steal away from her.

She looked at him, pensive and apprehensive.

"How do you see in me what I cannot sometimes?"

He smiled and took her face in his hand.

"Because I see you through the pain, past the anguish for the true and beautiful soul you are ... and I've never seen anything quite so amazing as the woman I see before me now."

She grinned shyly, for she wasn't used to such bold compliments.

It was in that moment that he saw a light peeking through her eyes that he had never noticed before ...

And that was when he knew.

She was finally starting to believe ...

In herself and in her love for him, and that was the most beautiful and fulfilling moment he had ever known ...

When she finally started to come home ...

To herself, to him, and to love.

She's Not an Ordinary Woman, So an Ordinary Love Will Never Do

The first time anyone meets her, they just know she's different.
She's rebuilt herself from broken hearts, broken roads and broken dreams.
She didn't have an easy past that led her to today, just the opposite.
She's fought, clawed and battled bravely to become the woman she wants to be ...
Never settling, never quitting, never losing hope.
She's more than just one of a kind, strong and resilient, and she's not one who will accept being treated disrespectfully or as just another option.
In fact, she's holding out for a love of the highest caliber – not because she needs companionship or love, but because she wants a love worth having.
One that will see her for who she is, what she's struggled to become and appreciate her ... all of her.
She's experienced all the wrong kinds of love, and she promised herself that she was done

letting undeserving people try to take up space in her heart.

People would tell her not to risk her heart for love because it never works out for anyone, but she shakes that off ...

She believes that true love exists, and she won't give up hope.

She refuses to sacrifice her morals, settle for anything less than the best or most of all, tolerate lackluster passion ... in herself or the ones close to her heart.

She knows her worth, loves herself and believes she can conquer the world on any given day.

Sure, she still has days that try to bring her down, but she's always going to be stronger than the worst storms that life throws at her.

So, when you cross her path, you won't ever forget seeing a woman of her quality.

She's proud, brave and strong in all the ways you may never know ...

But that's what makes her more than an everyday woman, much more than a one-of-a-kind person, but rather an immeasurable once-in-a-lifetime soul ...

She's not an everyday woman, and she'll never be okay with just an ordinary love ...

And she shows up every time with a smile on her face, a fire in her heart and passion in her soul.
That's the mark of an amazing woman.
Beautiful, strong and free.
She is and will always be ...
Unforgettable.

I've been ignoring what my heart has been whispering for too long ...
Telling me to stop standing still.
I'm not content any more to stay in one place, not moving forward and not growing.
I've let the struggles of life tear me down so far that I didn't even know if I could get back up ...
But I'm better than that, stronger than I once thought.
I've been down before and always managed to find my way, I just forgot how to pick myself up for a bit.
I'm done being stuck at rock bottom.
Those people who hurt me and let me down ... they don't control my path, I do.
Instead of looking back and wondering why they did what they did, I'm moving on and moving up.
Truth is, I'll never know why people who say they love you hurt you and leave, but sometimes, you have to be okay with that ...
And I'm learning that, day by day.
They chose their future by not including me and, now, I'm through standing still holding on to heartache and heartbreak.

Those misfortunes don't define me, and I'm not letting someone who's gone keep hurting me.
I can learn the lesson without harboring the pain ... and that's exactly what I'm going to do.
I'm pulling myself up out of rock bottom, and I'm clawing and fighting my way back to where I should have been all along.
No more wallowing, playing the victim or being content with people walking all over me.
I'm finding my voice, raising my fist and telling the world I'm taking back my life.
I'm done trying to convince people to love me, and I'm through with chasing partners who don't really want to love anyone but themselves.
It's time for me to rediscover my magic and fall back in love with myself.
That's what matters most of all.
Embracing my flaws, owning my choices and confronting my fears.
Stepping out and stepping up is a hard and scary thing to do, especially when you don't know where you're going ...
But I'm done being afraid of the future and the possibilities – I'm capable of so much more than I've let myself become.
That ends now.

I'm turning the page and starting fresh ... the past has nothing new to say, so I'm focused on what's ahead of me.

My life, my future and love for myself.

Anyone who can accept me for who I am and support me in my dreams, I welcome with open arms.

Forget the rest – I've listened to voices that tried to tell me what I can't do all my life.

This is my time ...

To shine, to breathe free and to start loving myself ...

And oh yes, Darling, it's my time to fly ...

And never look back.

When You Find Your People, Cherish Them

It wasn't until I was at my lowest points that I knew who my real friends were.

The people who stepped up and, without any hesitation, were there for me never letting me fall on my own.

That's when I knew who my tribe was – the beloved souls that had my back no matter what was going down ...

Sometimes, without even asking.

They listened to my heart when it was broken, and they stayed there and helped me put myself back together again.

I didn't ask them to stay, ask them to help or expect anything ...

They just did because that's what people who love you do.

They hold your hand when the world tries to take you down, letting you know that you're not alone and that they'll face the battles by your side.

They support me through my bad decisions, pick me up when I've fallen, and never stop loving me, even when I'm not very lovable sometimes.

The most beautiful part of those precious souls is that they do all those things because they want to – they love me, and they never judge or have conditions.

So, if you have those kinds of folks in your life, take the time and let them know what they mean to you.

Cherish them, love them and appreciate them ... not everyone is blessed like that.

If you need some people like that, go find some. Step out of your comfort zone and find the people like you – they're out there, waiting to embrace you ... you just haven't found them yet.

I know that I'm blessed when I can call someone at any time, day or night, and they're there for me.

Those are the ones who don't leave, don't hurt you and don't make you feel bad for having bad days and choosing terrible people to fall for.

Love those people with all your heart and never let them go.

One day, many years from now, you'll be glad you held onto those wonderful souls ...

Turn the moments with them into memories and tuck them away into your heart.

You'll be glad you did.

I Know My Worth

Darling,

I know that you think you know me, but I'm here to tell you that you have no clue ...

No clue what I've been through.

No clue about the fire I've walked through.

No clue how strong I am.

So, before you pass judgement on me and assume you know everything about me from a five-minute conversation, get to know me.

Try to understand just a little of where I've been, who I am and who I'm becoming before you think you know me.

Maybe I'm not the easiest person – I've built some high walls around my heart – but I'm worth every bit of time it will take you to earn my trust.

I have a huge heart and I'm passionate about my choices and my people – when I love, I do it with everything I have.

I don't do anything halfway, and I don't accept anything less than what I deserve.

Why?

Because I know what I'm worth, and I value myself and what I have to offer ...

I won't settle, be okay with disrespect or accept being just another option in your life.

If you want to love me – truly love me – then give me your honest, real and loyal love.

Don't play games or hold back ... I want to know all of you, because that's the only way this works – all of me and all of you.

There's going to be both ugly and beautiful parts, but that's just part of it.

Love isn't about seeing a perfect person but accepting an imperfect person perfectly.

I know what I want and what I'm good with, so if you want to earn my love, start with the parts that matter most:

My mind, heart and soul.

I'm worth it.

I've paid dearly for every ounce, and I own it.

Can you handle my truth?

The Worst Kind of Pain Is Getting Hurt by the Person You Explained Your Pain To

What hurts the most, as I think about those
painful words, isn't what you said ...
But rather who said them.
When our love was young and new, you told
me you'd never forsake me.
You promised me that you'd never leave me
and that you'd always stand beside me through
any storm.
I'd been hurt so many times before, and though
I didn't trust love,
You made me believe I could trust you enough
to take my walls down.
That you'd not break my heart like the ones
before.
I wanted to let you in to see the real me, to
finally have someone who saw and loved me
for me.
But in those few seconds when you turned
your back on me, everything that we had built –
and once believed in – came crashing down.
I never thought you'd be the one to break my
heart because you knew the journey I'd taken
to mend it.

You knew how scared I was to love again and, still, you decided to go instead of staying and trying to save us.

I can forgive you for so much, but never for leaving and giving up without fighting for love, for us.

There are no words that can comfort my ailing spirit and no light behind my eyes, for our once beautiful future has fallen into decay.

As I watched you walk away, I fought back the tears and struggled to keep it together.

Some people come into your life for a season, a reason or a lesson ...

You were all those things for me when I most needed to find a way to believe again.

In love, in hope ...

That maybe dreams can come true.

Yes, it hurt for a long time when you left – I may never truly get over you ...

But I know as more time passes, I will be grateful for you and what you taught me.

It doesn't mean it will be easy to accept or that the memories won't be painful,

But I'll realize the truth of what you showed me. It's okay to open your heart and believe in love, even if some people don't deserve or appreciate it.

It's up to us to figure out who truly is worth risking our hearts for.

While you weren't the one meant to be my person, you did show me the way to a healthier and happier me.

I guess I should thank you in the midst of my tears for setting me free.

Somewhere, someone else is looking for a love like mine.

That, for now, will be more than enough to make me smile ...

And find a way to believe again.

I Fall in Love with the People Who Look and Live Deeply

Give me the deep thinkers, the people who look past the surface and see what lies beyond.
I want to surround myself with the lovely ones who search for soulful connection and heartfelt feelings.
Why?
Because I'm one of them.
I need to feel the depth and meaning of life in ways that others do not ...
The mood behind the music, the feeling behind the lyrics ... I lose myself in the melodies and the rhythm permeates my soul.
Give me the songs of life and the deeper truths in everything, for those are the things that fill my spirit and put me at peace.
I want out of the ordinary and to seek the world that lies just out of sight, the beautiful mysteries of life that call out to be embraced.
That is who I am and what I need every day.
The adventure that evolves my thinking, the music that expands my consciousness and the love that sets my heart on fire.

Those are my people – the risk takers, the free thinkers, the ones who give their all in pursuit of passion, love and deep meanings.

I'll never be content with just existing and taking life at face value.

I need more ... much more.

To dive deeper into the things that move me, to immerse myself in amazing music, to uncover the parts of myself that I never knew existed.

I will live in the moment, search out the meanings and enjoy the beauty all around me.

You'll never find me sitting still or on the sidelines ...

Soulful, deep and passionate living, loving and laughing ... that's just who I am and what I love.

Take my hand.

Let's go chase some dreams and find some adventure.

Beautiful and free – just like us.

Let's make today a time to remember,

One moment at a time.

I Will Never Trade My Authenticity for Approval

Darling, if you think you're going to find another one like me, then you'll be sadly disappointed. I'd tell you they broke the mold after me, but I don't think there was ever a mold at all ...
I'm one of a kind.
I'll never be the one that you lose in a crowd, I'm the one overshadowing the crowd.
I have my own style, my own way of doing things, and I own every quirk that makes me unique.
I'm not trying to be different or stand out, I just shine brightly because I march to my own beat.
The world has always tried to scoff at me for my individuality, but what anyone thinks of me has never mattered in the least.
I don't need anyone's approval, permission or acceptance to be fabulous like I am.
I'm not seeking a spotlight because I shine from within, and no one can ever take that away from me.
Yeah, I'm a complete disaster sometimes and don't know where I'm going or why, but I always figure it out and own my mess ...
That's just part of my fantastic charisma ...

Doing what I want, how I want for the reasons that are all my own.

You'd be surprised how many people are scared of the ones like me who don't try to fit in.

They don't know what to make of me, and I don't expect them to.

I'm beautiful in the way that I choose, and I have a style that makes me happy ...

And that's what matters most: my own happiness.

Maybe the world will never understand me, and the crowds won't get me, but I'll always have my circle of friends who love me for every weird flaw and unique beauty that is me.

So, no, you'll never meet another soul like me, Darling – bold, daring and audacious.

I love my life, and I spread my sunshine everywhere I go.

And one thing is for certain:

I'll never trade my authenticity for anyone's approval.

Try as you might, you'll never find awesomeness better than me.

I'm not the candle in the wind you may have been hoping for ...

I'm the bold loving soul who will set your night on fire ...
And I'm not holding back.

She'll Gather the Best of Her and Then She'll Simply Walk Away

She's fallen apart before, so this time is no different.

She'll pull herself together, pick up the pieces she needs and begin to rebuild herself like she always has.

Broken hearts and lost loves are no stranger to her, she's waded through the seas of her discontent many times before.

It's the risk she knows she faces when she chooses to love, for she loves with all her heart and gives it her all.

She doesn't do anything halfway and passion fills her soul as she seeks love ...

So, as she picks up the shattered pieces of her heart, she knows this lonely road all too well.

It aches to her deepest places, but that's the price she's accustomed to paying for loving the way she does ... and she wouldn't change a thing about who she is and the choices she makes.

She'll never stop believing in happily ever after and true love, so she long ago made peace with the road to happiness.

She learns something from every dead end
and tries to grow each time.
She'll pick up the pieces she needs to move on
and move up, leaving behind the parts of the
past that don't serve her anymore ...
She knows that to truly evolve, she must let go
of the baggage that used to weigh her down
and open the doors to new possibilities.
Her friends tell her she's strong and brave, not
that she sees that in herself.
She just sees a woman with a broken past
trying to build a brighter future as she picks up
the pieces along the way to forge her armor.
She didn't choose this path, for she had no
other choice ...
She just kept pushing forward, kept believing,
kept loving like she does.
So, when the darkness of broken love tries to
bring her down, she shrugs it off and keeps
moving.
She knows this challenging road ... and nothing
on it will ever bring her down.
Living, laughing and loving with all her heart
will always be her way ...
And as she picks up the pieces from a lost
love, she just smiles and laughs.
"Not today, sadness ... not ever."

With one last look, she shakes her head and turns her face to the sunlight.
Some souls were just meant to shine brighter ... so that's exactly what she kept doing ... brighter than the night sky.

For so long I spent every bit of my heart on the
people that I loved.
I love my people deeply because that's who I
am ... and that's not going to change.
But I never realized that I while I was using all
of my energy on everyone else, I never left
anything for myself.
I would always put others before myself
because I'm a person who loves to see others
happy.
But those same friends helped me understand
that I deserve that same love too ... that I was
worthy of loving myself in a way that I had
ignored for too long.
Truthfully, it's easier to avoid parts of yourself
when you're focused on others ...
And when I chose to give the best parts of me
to me, I came face to face with my own truths –
some wonderful and some not as pretty.
I had to confront the things I had ignored,
avoided and even buried as I projected my
focus onto others.

I'll never change my giving heart, but I know now that I must love myself first ... all of me, or I'm lying to myself and not being honest.

Oh, I know it's not always going to be easy, and there'll be days when I don't want to face it. But that's just part of my journey.

There's only one way through the pain and the past, and it's straight through.

I'll stumble and fall, cry in frustration and want to pull my hair out, but I know this is the only way I will ever be able to truly love all of myself the way I've always deserved.

More than that, I can love my people and my partner with a greater passion than I've ever had ... a love born of peace and letting go.

So, here's to making peace with the pain, finding a way through the hard stuff and learning how to finally love myself fully.

It may be messy and harder than I realize, but I can do this.

With love in my heart, fire in my soul and an iron will,

There's nothing that I can't do.

She Will Rise

She's finally hit the point where she's done with it all.

She's done with people letting her down, trying to disrespect her and hurt her.

No more.

She has been beaten down and hit rock bottom, but she's not staying there.

She's been lost for too long, and it's her time now.

She's rising up from the ashes with the courage of a thousand warriors and the roar of a million lions.

No longer will she accept failure, mistakes and struggle.

She's been trapped in the fires of life for too long, and she's choosing to become more.

She's the Phoenix and cannot be stopped.

She will rise up above those who would see her fail.

Bruises, dents and scratches won't dissuade her from pushing forward and rising up.

Her veins are coursing with a fiery passion that fills her spirit, and she won't be denied.

She's been put off and disregarded for far too long.

She's turning the page, setting her world ablaze and taking back her life.

Pain from her past is the fuel for her ascent, and she's on fire with an undeniable hunger to rise above, to succeed and to start realizing her dreams.

Those words that used to define her ... "can't," "won't," "shouldn't" ... those are forgotten, never to be uttered again.

The world has never seen a creature like her with an indomitable drive to find her wings and fly higher than she ever knew she could.

She's leaving behind the haters, the jealous, the disbelievers, and anyone else who won't stand by her side as she fights her way to the top.

She knows what she deserves, and she's not settling for anything less than what she wants.

She's waited her entire life for this chance to become who she was always meant to be.

No more second guessing, hesitation or questions.

She's doing what she has to do to push through and fight for her dreams.

It won't be easy – her life never has been – but she will never quit.

She's more than a warrior, a strong woman or
a lioness.
She is a Phoenix rising,
And her time is now.

Together We Rise

Ravenwolf

Find more love, hope and empowerment at
www.houseofravenwolf.com
including Ravenwolf's complete works
and quote merchandise.

Keep rising!